A. PHILIP RANDOLPH

*Integration in
the Workplace*

The History of the
Civil Rights Movement

A. PHILIP RANDOLPH

Integration in the Workplace

by **Sarah Wright**

With an Introduction by
ANDREW YOUNG

Silver Burdett Press

To my beloved ones, my granddaughter and my husband,
Amy Chotai and Joseph Kaye

Series Consultant: Aldon Morris

Cover and Text Design: Design Five, New York
Maps: General Cartography, Inc.
Series Editorial Supervisor: Richard G. Gallin
Series Supervision of Art and Design: Leslie Bauman
Series Editing: Agincourt Press
Developmental Editor: Della Rowland

Consultants: Glennette Tilley Turner, Educator and author, Wheaton, Illinois;
Fath Ruffins, Historian, National Museum of American History, Smithsonian
Institution, Washington, D.C.

Library of Congress Cataloging-in-Publication Data

Wright, Sarah E.
A. Philip Randolph: integration in the workplace / by Sarah Wright; with an
introduction by Andrew Young.
    p.   cm. —(The History of the civil rights movement)
    Includes bibliographical references and index.
    Summary: A biography of the civil rights activist who organized
the Brotherhood of Sleeping Car Porters, which acted as a labor
union for Pullman car porters.
    1. Randolph, A. Philip (Asa Philip), 1889–   —Juvenile
literature.   2. Afro-Americans—Biography—Juvenile literature.
3. Civil rights workers—United States—Biography—Juvenile
literature.   4. Brotherhood of Sleeping Car Porters—History-
Juvenile literature.   5. Civil rights movements—United States-
-History—20th century—Juvenile literature.   6. Afro-Americans-
-Civil rights—Juvenile literature. [1. Randolph, A. Philip (Asa
Philip), 1889–   . 2. Civil rights workers.   3. Afro-Americans-
Biography.]   I. Title.   II. Series.
E185.97.R72W75   1990
323'.092—dc20
[B]
[92]
ISBN 0-382-09922-2 (lib bdg.)
ISBN 0-382-24059-6 (pbk.)
                                                          90-31787
                                                          CIP
                                                          AC

CONTENTS

INTRODUCTION

By Andrew Young

Some thirty years ago, a peaceful revolution took place in the United States, as African Americans sought equal rights. That revolution, which occurred between 1954 and 1968, is called the civil rights movement. Actually, African Americans have been struggling for their civil rights for as long as they have been in this country. Before the Civil War, brave abolitionists were calling out for an end to the injustice and cruelty of slavery. Even after the Civil War freed slaves, African Americans were still forced to fight other forms of racism and discrimination—segregation and prejudice. This movement still continues today as people of color battle racial hatred and economic exploitation all over the world.

The books in this series tell the stories of the lives of Ella Baker, Stokely Carmichael, Fannie Lou Hamer, Jesse Jackson, Malcolm X, Thurgood Marshall, Rosa Parks, A. Philip Randolph, and Martin Luther King, Jr.—just a few of the thousands of brave people who worked in the civil rights movement. Learning about these heroes is an important lesson in American history. They risked their homes and their jobs—and some gave their lives—to secure rights and freedoms that we now enjoy and often take for granted.

Most of us know the name of Dr. Martin Luther King, Jr., the nonviolent leader of the movement. But others who were just as important may not be as familiar. Rosa Parks insisted on her right to a seat on a public bus. Her action started a bus boycott that changed a segregation law and sparked a movement.

Ella Baker was instrumental in founding two major civil rights organizations, the Southern Christian Leadership Conference (SCLC) and the Student Nonviolent Coordinating Committee (SNCC). One of the chairpersons of SNCC, Stokely Carmichael, is perhaps best known for making the slogan "Black Power" famous. Malcolm X, the strong voice from the urban north, rose from a prison inmate to a powerful black Muslim leader.

Not many people know that the main organizer of the 1963 March on Washington was A. Philip Randolph. Younger leaders called Randolph the "father of the movement." Fannie Lou Hamer, a poor sharecropper from Mississippi, was such a powerful speaker for voters rights that President Lyndon Johnson blocked out television coverage of the 1964 Democratic National Convention to keep her off the air. Thurgood Marshall was the first African American to be made a Supreme Court justice.

Many who demanded equality paid for their actions. They were fired from their jobs, thrown out of their homes, beaten, and even killed. But they marched, went to jail, and put their lives on the line over and over again for the right to equal justice. These rights include something as simple as being able to sit and eat at a lunch counter. They include political rights such as the right to vote. They also include the equal rights to education and job opportunities that lead to economic betterment.

We are now approaching a level of democracy that allows all citizens of the United States to participate in the American dream. Jesse Jackson, for example, has pursued the dream of the highest office in this land, the president of the United States. Jackson's running for president was made possible by those who went before him. They are the people whose stories are included in this biography and history series, as well as thousands of others who remain nameless. They are people who depend upon you to carry on the dream of liberty and justice for all people of the world.

Civil Rights Movement Time Line

——1954———1955———1956———1957——

May 17—
Brown v. Board of Education of Topeka I: Supreme Court rules racial segregation in public is unconstitutional.

May 31—
Brown v. Board of Education of Topeka II: Supreme Court says desegregation of public schools must proceed "with all deliberate speed."

August 28—
14-year-old Emmett Till is killed in Money, Mississippi.

December 5, 1955–December 20, 1956—
Montgomery, Alabama bus boycott.

November 13—
Supreme Court outlaws racial segregation on Alabama's city buses.

January 10, 11—
Southern Christian Leadership Conference (SCLC) is founded.

August 29—
Civil Rights Act is passed. Among other things, it creates Civil Rights Commission to advise the president and gives government power to uphold voting rights.

September 1957—
Little Rock Central High School is desegregated.

——1962———1963———1964——

September 29—
Federal troops help integrate University of Mississippi ("Ole Miss") after two people are killed and several are injured.

April to May—
Birmingham, Alabama, demonstrations. School children join the marches.

May 20—
Supreme Court rules Birmingham's segregation laws are unconstitutional.

June 12—
NAACP worker Medgar Evers is killed in Jackson, Mississippi.

August 28—
March on Washington draws more than 250,000 people.

September 15—
Four girls are killed when a Birmingham church is bombed.

November 22—
President John F. Kennedy is killed in Dallas, Texas.

March–June—
St. Augustine, Florida, demonstrations.

June 21—
James Chaney, Michael Schwerner, and Andrew Goodman are killed while registering black voters in Mississippi.

July 2—
Civil Rights Act is passed. Among other things, it provides for equal job opportunities and gives the government power to sue to desegregate public schools and facilities.

August—
Mississippi Freedom Democratic Party (MFDP) attempts to represent Mississippi at the Democratic National Convention.

2

—1958———1959———1960———1961—

September 1958–August 1959—
Little Rock Central High School is closed because governor refuses to integrate it.

February 1—
Student sit-ins at lunch counter in Greensboro, North Carolina, begin sit-in protests all over the South.

April 17—
Student Nonviolent Coordinating Committee (SNCC) is founded.

May 6—
Civil Rights Act is passed. Among other things, it allows judges to appoint people to help blacks register to vote.

Eleven African countries win their independence.

May 4—
Freedom Rides leave Washington, D.C., and head south.

September 22—
Interstate Commerce Commission ordered to enforce desegregation laws on buses, and trains, and in travel facilities like waiting rooms, rest rooms, and restaurants.

—1965———1966———1967———1968—

January–March—
Selma, Alabama, demonstrations.

February 21—
Malcolm X is killed in New York City.

March 21–25—
More than 25,000 march from Selma to Montgomery, Alabama.

August 6—
Voting Rights Act passed.

August 11–16—
Watts riot (Los Angeles, California).

June—
James Meredith "March Against Fear" from Memphis, Tennessee, to Jackson, Mississippi. Stokely Carmichael makes slogan "Black Power" famous during march.

Fall—
Black Panther Party for Self-Defense is formed by Huey Newton and Bobby Seale in Oakland, California.

June 13—
Thurgood Marshall is appointed first African-American U.S. Supreme Court justice.

Summer—
Riots break out in 30 U.S. cities.

April 4—
Martin Luther King, Jr., is killed in Memphis, Tennessee.

April 11—
Civil Rights Act is passed. Among other things, it prohibits discrimination in selling and renting houses or apartments.

May 13–June 23—
Poor People's March: Washington, D.C., to protest poverty.

1 ASA ENTERS THE WORLD

> **❝ I've been rebuked and I've been scorned. ❞**
>
> "Hell and Heaven,"
> African-American
> folk song

It was 20 years past slavery times when James William Randolph came to Baldwin, Florida, to be a preacher. Good-looking and tall, 20-year-old Randolph was sure of his path. For he had been schooled and trained in southern Florida by northern missionaries, people who were sent by religious groups to spread their beliefs. Randolph was going to lift the hopes of the terribly poor people of his new community. He was going to ask them to share their troubles with him, for troubles they surely had. It was no easy thing being an African American in 1884, especially not in the South.

Randolph led the services of his small African Methodist Episcopal (AME) church. He taught the Sunday school classes, too, where he met a serious and charming girl just entering her teens, Elizabeth Robinson.

Elizabeth was beautiful, strong of character, and clear-minded. Perhaps she had inherited her high forehead and cheekbones from her mother, who was half-black, half-Native American. Or perhaps they had come from her fiery father, who looked white but let it be known with pride that he was African American. He was a man who made his living by buying and selling lumber, and he grew more prosperous each year as he put up more and more buildings to store the lumber. As he prospered, he became more and more proud of the ever-growing signs of his worth. He bowed to no man and always carried a gun to silence anyone who might dare to speak to him without the proper respect.

The new preacher, with his handsome face, silvery voice, and beautiful thoughts, stirred Elizabeth's love for God and for the man of God. James fell in love with her in turn, and they were married within a year.

The Randolphs had very little money. But somehow, James managed to scrape enough together to buy many fine books, which were kept in their library. James Randolph not only read many of the best English writers, whom he especially liked— Shakespeare, Charles Dickens, Jane Austen, Keats, and Shelley—but he also kept up with the writings of his own people. He studied the history of his church. He eagerly read the black newspapers and journals, such as the *Christian Recorder,* the *AME Review,* and the *Voice of the Negro.*

Elizabeth shared completely the interests of her husband. With a keen intelligence, she learned quickly. They both felt that education was the key to their personal development and the key to the advancement of their people.

In May 1887, the birth of their first child, James William, Jr., took place. A few months later, the Randolphs moved to Crescent City, another small town in Florida, where their second child, Asa Philip Randolph, was born on April 15, 1889.

Why had they named him Asa? In the Bible, Asa was a kind and generous king who had given up all his wealth to protect his people from foreign invasion. He ended up a poor man, but he won the war and kept his people free.

Trying to support a growing family and obeying a decision of his church, James Randolph moved them to Jacksonville, Florida, a larger town where there was a better chance to earn more money. But even there, those who came to the church could not give him enough for his family to live on. James had to go up and down the St. Johns River preaching to other groups of churchgoers, as well. Many times the people could only pay him with a sack of potatoes. But he kept going. For he was serving God and God's people.

James Randolph was trying to follow in the footsteps of the Reverend Richard Allen. In the late 18th century, Allen had been ordered to leave a Methodist Episcopal church in Philadelphia because he would not move from the place reserved for whites. So he went out and, with another black minister, set up a new church, the first African Methodist Episcopal Church. The church became very active in the cause of helping to end slavery and the shameful treatment of blacks, in the North as well as in the South. AME churches were set up throughout the country. Randolph was happy in such a church, one that was both a praying church and a fighting church.

When the 13th Amendment to the U.S. Constitution had officially ended slavery, in 1865, black people thought that a wonderful new day was dawning for them. A time called Reconstruction began in the South. Reconstruction meant building a new southern way of life. For over 200 years, blacks had been forced to work with the whip. Their bodies belonged to the slave masters who could do whatever they wanted with their slaves. For over 200 years, they worked for no pay. Now black people were free. They could work for whomever they wanted and be paid. The 14th Amendment to the U.S. Constitution, in 1868, gave ex-slaves full citizenship and protection. It said the states had to give them the right to vote. The 15th Amendment to the U.S. Constitution, in 1870, said that neither the U.S. government nor the states could prevent men from voting because of their race or color or because they had once been slaves.

In the years right after the Civil War, many blacks helped make laws in the southern states. They saw to it that free public schools were set up for blacks and whites together. Before Reconstruction, there were laws in the South forbidding public education for blacks. In the southern states in the old days, the governments only protected the slave owners. Under Reconstruction, the governments were supposed to help everybody, including the 4 million blacks who were freed and poor whites. But Reconstruction did not last past 1877. The former slave owners and their friends wanted things the way they were before. They could not make blacks their slaves again, but they did everything they could to keep black people down.

Beginning in 1881, southern state legislatures passed laws forbidding black people to ride in railway cars used by white people. These laws spread to every public place, including schools and hospitals. This separation, called segregation, was intended to support the idea that the white race was superior. The segregation laws were called Jim Crow laws. The North did not pass such laws, but it did practice racial segregation.

The days of hope had ended. Randolph saw that now things were going back to the old ways, little by little. The former slave owners spread terror across the South. Several thousand African Americans were killed when they tried to stand up for their rights. The former slave owners stole the elections by not counting the black votes. Then blacks and poor whites were no longer allowed to hold office or even vote. Laws were passed to keep the races separate, segregated. Funds for schooling were cut back. Poor farmers, black and white, but especially black, were forced into a new kind of oppression called sharecropping.

African Americans were granted the right to vote in 1870, as illustrated in Harper's Weekly.

Sharecropping came about when the slaves were set free. Because they were given no land, they were forced to work for others. Under this system, the landowner let the sharecroppers use his land and also lent them mules, tools, and seed to plant crops. In return, the sharecroppers had to give to the landowner about half of what was grown, usually cotton. When the sharecroppers needed to buy food, clothing, and other essentials, they had to go to the landowner's store. At the end of the year, the landowner would often lie to the sharecroppers about how much was owed him for these purchases. Sharecroppers would then have to turn over most of the remaining crop to the landowner in order to pay their debts. Year after year, no matter how hard the sharecroppers worked, they usually ended up owing the landowner more money.

If the sharecroppers tried to stand up for their rights, they were sometimes killed by mobs. When the mobs killed someone, it was called a lynching. And one of the favorite ways of lynching black people was to tie a rope around their necks and hang them from a tree. Almost 2,000 African Americans were lynched during the years when James Randolph was growing up.

Things in Jacksonville were a little better than they were in many other places in the South. There was an integrated library where people of both races could use the books. The races could also ride together on public transportation. The police department had a few black employees, and one of the chief judges in the city was black. Still, the situation was very bad. Most African Americans were desperately poor and had little chance to overcome their poverty. Few even thought about going on to college or even high school.

What was to be done? What could a minister say to his people? They needed to be paid more money. But to ask for more money might cause them to be beaten or even killed. Who would be brave enough to stand up to the powerful whites?

One day, four black men came to the Randolph home. Asa was only a boy then, about nine years old. He never forgot what happened. Many years later, he would tell the story of how these men had given his father the news that a black man was being held in the town jail. His father was warned that some white people were getting ready to take the man out of the jail and lynch him. James Randolph then said something to his wife in a low voice, and grabbing a shotgun, marched out of the house with the men. Standing in the kitchen, Asa's mother had taken out another shotgun and loaded it. The Reverend James Randolph had been gone the whole night while his wife, Elizabeth, stood guard over the boys and the house. Finally, at dawn, he had come home, smiling.

Over breakfast, James Randolph told how he and 11 other black men had gone over to the jail and waited with their guns.

He told how a group of whites had come later on to carry out the lynching. And then Randolph laughed when he described the look on those white folks' faces when they saw a dozen armed black men standing in their way. Those white men suddenly remembered they had something else to do and left the jail in a big rush. There was no lynching that night in Jacksonville.

Asa would never forget the bravery of his father and his mother. He armed himself with that bravery, and it served him the rest of his life. He would surely need it!

SCHOOL DAYS

> ❝ *Walk together children,* *don't you get weary.* ❞

"Walk Together Children,"
African-American spiritual

The two Randolph boys could not bear to be apart. When James, Jr., started school, Asa went right along with him. James, Jr., was very quick in his studies, easily making A's, and he taught Asa whatever he learned.

When they came home from school, their father would sit down with them, take one of the books from his library, and read to them. The boys eagerly soaked up the new worlds being opened up to them.

Another thing that they learned from their father was his

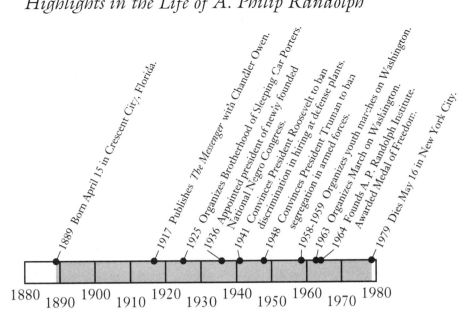

1889 Born April 15 in Crescent City, Florida.

1917 Publishes *The Messenger* with Chandler Owen.

1925 Organizes Brotherhood of Sleeping Car Porters.

1936 Appointed president of newly founded National Negro Congress.

1941 Convinces President Roosevelt to ban discrimination in hiring at defense plants.

1948 Convinces President Truman to ban segregation in armed forces.

1958-1959 Organizes youth marches on Washington.

1963 Organizes March on Washington.

1964 Founds A. P. Randolph Institute. Awarded Medal of Freedom.

1979 Dies May 16 in New York City.

1880 1890 1900 1910 1920 1930 1940 1950 1960 1970 1980

wonderful speaking style, which he had developed over the years as a preacher. He could say the words perfectly, he seemed to know every word in the dictionary, and he could make his voice travel all the way to the back of an auditorium. The boys were impressed, too, with his dignified manner and the way he had of standing so straight. Both boys wanted to grow up to be just like him.

Their mother usually kept busy with gardening or tailoring to try to make some extra money. Sometimes Asa and James helped her out in the garden. They raised collard greens, tomatoes, strawberries, peas, and chickens. Even so, it was always a hard struggle to make enough money to buy the simple things they needed.

Tailoring was also to their father's liking. He had been trained as a tailor by the northern missionaries in the same school where he learned to be a preacher. It was a skill he never forgot. But no matter how skillful he was, he could not make it pay well enough. His clients were too poor, and he was too kindhearted to charge them what he should have or to insist upon being paid when they said they didn't have any money. Elizabeth was the firm one in the business. Her attitude was, "No money, no clothes."

Elizabeth did not go out much socially, except to see neighbors and friends at weddings or funerals. She spent her time taking care of the home and devoting herself to community work through the church.

Those were precious years in the lives of James, Jr., and Asa. James, Jr., continued to do well in school. Even though he was serious and quiet, he enjoyed sports, as did Asa. From time to time, James, Jr., was forced to defend himself in fights after school, usually because some boys were jealous of his and Asa's high grades. When some bully attacked James, Jr., Asa would rush to help him. Sometimes they were both badly beaten, and sometimes they got the better of their attackers.

When they came home cut and bruised from these fights, instead of scolding them and telling them not to fight, their mother praised them for standing up for themselves, and encouraged them to learn the art of self-defense.

One day, Asa learned that a few white men a thousand miles away had decided something that would have a terrible effect on African-American people for the rest of Asa's life. It was 1896, and in Washington, D.C., the Supreme Court—the highest court in the land—decided in a case called *Plessy* v. *Ferguson* (*v.* means "against") that black children could be forced to go to separate schools and could be kept out of parks where white children played. The Court upheld the Jim Crow laws that had been passed by the southern state governments. Blacks could be kept out of stores, restaurants, theaters, hotels, wherever whites didn't want them. This segregation was the opposite of integration. It seemed that what the Court was really saying was that whites were better than blacks, and that since African-Americans were not worth as much as whites, they could be paid less, could be given less education and fewer rights.

The Randolph family was very angry when they got this

news. They could never accept it. Asa would spend the rest of his life fighting that decision.

It wasn't long before Asa's enthusiasm for learning ran up against this growing trend against equal rights for African Americans. Asa had read most of the books in the family library and wanted to read more. So he went to the public library where he knew there were thousands of books that would help him travel up the road to higher knowledge. Asa could hardly contain his excitement as he pushed open the heavy library door. He fairly ran to the librarian's desk to ask about getting a library card. Within thirty seconds he was back outside the building again, his cheeks burning, the ugly words ringing in his ears. The librarian had told him that the library was no place for blacks.

Asa ran home, choking back his tears. His father would straighten things out. He was sure of it.

Asa waited. But his father did not straighten things out, could not straighten them out. A tide was sweeping through the state, through the South, through the country, a tide that even Asa's beloved father could not stop.

Still, there were happy moments for Asa, as when he was taken by his father on trips up the great St. Johns River. Then he would see ships and boats of all kinds moving up and down the water. He would watch people trading all sorts of goods. Everyone was on the move. There were people of every skin shade, and many languages: European languages, such as French and Spanish, and languages of different Native American tribes.

The Reverend James Randolph would stop and preach in out-of-the-way places where few people lived. It was not always easy to find these places, especially in the dark, but Asa's father never got lost, even on the darkest night. When they reached a village, they would be happily greeted with sayings like, "God bless your soul," and then always, "Come right in and eat." The happy way the people fussed over them was enough to make anyone feel pretty special. But they felt even more so when their father introduced them with words like "These are my boys, and they are two of the finest boys in the world!"

The Reverend James Randolph prayed. He talked to his God. He looked for a sign, a way out. But things kept getting worse.

Then came the notices in the local newspapers. They informed black people that from now on they would be allowed to sit only at the back of buses and other public means of transportation. They had to give up their seats to white people if they needed them.

The news swept through the African-American community like a fire out of control. People were confused, uncertain about what to do. But not the Reverend James Randolph. He told his sons under no circumstances would his family use segregated public transportation. From now on, they would walk—and walk they did. Thus, Asa took his first steps on his long journey to end racial discrimination.

3 WHICH ROAD TO TRAVEL?

***" The trumpet sounds within my soul. "*"**

"Steal Away,"
African-American
spiritual

Sixteen-year-old James, Jr., now began attending the Cookman Institute, and Asa, two years younger, tagged right along with him. Cookman was a combination of high school and junior college and was run by Methodists from the North. It was the only school of higher education available for black youngsters in the Jacksonville area. The Randolph boys needed to keep that in mind and be grateful. So few black children could go beyond elementary school. The Freedmen's Bureau had been set up by the United States Congress after the Civil War in 1865. Its job was to help feed, protect, and educate the former slaves. The bureau set up 4,000 schools and brought in teachers. But that was not enough. Then, in 1877, when Reconstruction ended, the bureau was closed down anyway. Those who took control after Reconstruction did not believe much in education, not for farmers, not for poor whites, and certainly not for blacks. They allowed only a very few higher schools for African Americans to be built. But even when they were built, there was very little money to pay the teachers. So the boys were lucky indeed to be able to study at Cookman.

Once in a while there would be news about a university being set up for African Americans, such as Howard University in Washington, D.C., or Fisk University in Nashville, Tennessee. Such news was always met with joy in Asa's home. It would help the boys forget their aching feet from the long daily walks to and from school. The universities gave them hope.

Their father would always tell them that they *could* be somebody. To his father, Asa seemed just right to follow in his footsteps and become a minister, while James, Jr., could become a lawyer and fight for his people in the courts. He might even be a judge. Their mother, too, always had words of encouragement.

It was good to be believed in, but Asa felt a growing weight on him as he realized how much his family counted on his carrying on the family preaching tradition. For Asa had begun to question things, a lot of things. He had begun by questioning why black people were treated the way they were. His father had taught him to do that. This had led him not to accept anything at face value, not to accept things just because people said they were so, or because powerful people said you must.

Asa now began to apply this questioning frame of mind even to the Bible. He prayed for understanding, at his father's instructions. Somehow he just couldn't accept the idea that all the Bible stories were true. Asa was afraid to tell his parents about these doubts. They might have a heart attack or a stroke, he thought. He'd even heard of people dying of a broken heart.

Asa knew he was going to do something worthwhile, but

preaching—was that the way? A book in his father's library called *The Souls of Black Folk* led him to think about another way. That book, written in 1903 by the great African-American leader W.E.B. Du Bois, inspired Asa and made him more determined than ever to amount to something. Du Bois had written that the African-American race, like all races, was going to be saved by its very special people. He called these the "talented tenth," and he said they would lead their people to freedom. Was not he, Asa, one of those in the "talented tenth"?

When Asa was about 16, he began organizing. He began to gather small groups of students around him. He read to them from the books that had inspired him. He had spent so many hours reading Shakespeare and the Bible that it was a pleasure to be able to share them. He especially loved the story of Jesus' disciple Paul because it portrayed a man of loyalty, endurance, and courage. Asa saw that he had a great hold over his au-

W. E. B. Du Bois had a profound effect on A. Philip Randolph's intellectual growth.

diences, that he was able to move them, that his voice had great power. Added to all that was Asa's good looks.

Asa began toying with the idea of becoming an actor on the stage. He would bring his friends together and put on dramatic pieces at various social get-togethers in the community. While everyone was impressed with his acting, it was his voice that people liked most. A voice like a deep bell, they said.

In his spare time, Asa practiced pronouncing words in what sounded to his ears like the perfect English style that he so admired. He practiced walking and standing as straight as he could, with his head up, just like his father, so that he could convey the idea "I am somebody!"

When he spoke before people, he always got an encouraging response. But the audience's greatest excitement came when he spoke about the terrible crimes being daily committed against the millions of black men, women, and children. When he spoke about these things and how the outrage of lynchings always went unpunished, his eyes would blaze and his voice would ring out. And the people in the audience would give back to him the same strong feelings.

Asa was so good at so many things that he didn't know which direction to take. He was an excellent student, and with his brother, was at the top of his classes. He even found time to play basketball and became one of the stars on his school team. Their classmates held the Randolph boys in awe, but the boys did not let this go to their heads.

Naturally, their teachers took a special interest in them— Lillie Whitney and Mary Neff, in particular, who had come from the North to teach black children. They helped deepen Asa's love for the poems of the great English writers John Keats, Lord Byron, and Percy Bysshe Shelley, the novels of Charles Dickens and Jane Austen—writers whom Asa's father had introduced him to earlier. Asa also was taught about the great black poet Phillis Wheatley.

Asa not only studied Latin, mathematics, history, and science—subjects that were usually taught only to white children—but he also carefully read the daily newspaper *The Clarion-Ledger*. He wanted to keep in touch with what was happening to his people around the country. He didn't have to pay for the paper, since he and his brother had jobs delivering it all over the black sections of Jacksonville.

As they walked the several miles of their paper route every day, they played a game of remembering black history. It went something like this:

Asa might ask: "Who was the first man to die in the American Revolution?"

James would shout his answer: "Crispus Attucks." Then he would ask Asa to name three slaves who led revolts. Asa could usually answer his brother's questions. And he certainly knew about Nat Turner, Denmark Vesey, and Gabriel Prosser.

Most of the time James would win, but by testing each other, both would learn more.

Little by little, Asa caught up with James and then surpassed him in many subjects. So it came as no surprise when Asa Philip Randolph graduated at the head of his class in 1907. He was called the valedictorian. He was chosen to give the graduation speech. Its title was "The Man of the Hour." In his speech, Asa spoke about the ideas of W.E.B. Du Bois. He told his classmates that it was the duty of those lucky enough to have skills and knowledge to lead their people out of their suffering. He urged those few who would be going to the universities to use their education to help their people.

It was this suffering that drove hundreds of thousands of African Americans to look for a better life in the North. But the Reverend James Randolph refused to leave. He felt his duty lay with those who remained, with those who faced the full fury of southern racism, with those who faced the misery of southern terror and hopelessness.

All over the South, laws were being passed to take rights away from black people. But in the North as well as the South, African Americans were being made fun of in books and magazines, in songs, and on the stage. Black people were depicted as stupid and childish or as dangerous animals. In the North as well as the South, blacks were given the dirtiest, the most dangerous, and the poorest-paid jobs— when they were lucky enough to find jobs. Black people were not permitted to take what was called "white man's work." They were not allowed to join labor unions. They were forced to live in ghettos, where they were overcrowded in rundown houses and where they had to pay more for the houses than they were worth.

After high-school graduation, Asa got a job collecting money from people who had bought life insurance. It was a dull job. But his mind was not on his job anyway. In his spare time, he started a drama club. He began to feel that he could help his people by becoming a famous actor. If whites saw how a black man could become a great actor, maybe blacks would win more respect. He wanted to talk to his parents about this.

He wanted to talk to his parents about a lot of things, but he knew they were still hoping he would become a minister. Asa had by now made up his mind that the ministry was not for him. He knew his brother felt the same way.

One Sunday, as usual, the Reverend James Randolph called on all the sinners in the church to change their ways and to turn to God and to be welcomed into the arms of the church. Asa and James, Jr., who had been sitting in the last row, suddenly jumped up and started shouting and moaning. They then walked down to the mourner's bench at the very front of the church. In front of the whole congregation, they fell on their knees and prayed for God to forgive their sins. They said they were going to devote their lives to the church.

What a wonderful moment of joy for the Randolph family! At long last, their boys had seen the light.

It was a good thing, however, that the minister and his wife could not read the thoughts of their two boys. It was a very good thing that they had not seen the winks and smiles the boys had exchanged just before they went down the church aisle. For they had only been pretending. It was a cruel joke on their parents. Yes, they were good boys, but they were not perfect.

4 ASA MAKES A DECISION

> ❝ *To thine own self be true.* ❞
>
> **WILLIAM SHAKESPEARE,**
> *Hamlet*

Asa had for a long time been curious about the North. So when the chance came along to visit the North, especially that famous Harlem, in New York City, the black capital of the United States, he grabbed it.

When Asa was 17, still in school and on summer vacation, his cousin who was living in New York found him a job helping him clean an apartment house on 89th Street in Manhattan. Asa swept and mopped the floors. He remembered reading that many hotels had signs saying, "George Washington Slept Here." So one afternoon, on the corner of a staircase he was cleaning, he carved, "A.P. Randolph Swept Here."

That summer sped by for Asa. Impressions of the fast-moving city pressed in on him from all sides. He needed time to figure things out. How strange everything was, and yet how familiar. People were in such a hurry—in a hurry to get to work and in a hurry to get home from work. They were even in a hurry on their day off. That was strange to Asa. But the poverty of his people, seeing them working as cooks and porters and cleaning people, this was all too familiar to him.

It seemed everyone in Harlem came from one southern state or another. Every once in a while, he'd even find someone who came from Jacksonville, and they would talk about the people they both knew.

Asa understood there were no laws in New York preventing black people from going where they wanted, as there were in Florida. But Asa saw that actually there were many places where black people did not go. They did not go to the hotels downtown or many of the restaurants. It seemed as if most jobs were closed to them.

Yes, they could vote, but it didn't seem to make much of a difference, except that once in a while a black person might be able to get a small favor from a politician.

Asa couldn't make up his mind whether he was disappointed in New York or not. He guessed he'd have to come back again and find out more.

At the end of that summer, Asa went back to Jacksonville, back to life in the South. From what Asa heard and read in the papers, Jacksonville was still a lot better off than most other places in the South. The worst horrors took place in the areas of the large plantations, especially in Mississippi, Louisiana, Georgia, and Alabama. This was called the Black Belt, where the big landowners ruled with an iron hand.

But how little black life meant to whites even in Jacksonville was truly brought home at the time of the great fire in 1901. It had happened so suddenly, and once it got started, nothing could stop it. The fire had roared through Jacksonville, racing through more than 150 blocks of the city, or about a third of the total area. Hundreds of houses were destroyed and thousands of people were left homeless.

Asa could understand that the fire was an accident and no one's fault. But the special suffering of the black people was no accident. Asa watched in rising anger as the white firefighters fought to keep the flames from spreading in the white sections of the city but refused to fight the fire when it crossed into the black sections. The black people were running back and forth with small buckets of water, throwing them against the huge fire. It was not helping, but they kept doing it anyhow. Asa saw the hurt expressions on their faces as everything they owned turned to ashes.

But the black community did not give way to despair. Asa's father and mother, along with many other families up and down his street, opened up their homes and took in those who had been burned out. Nobody had that much extra space to begin with. But they shared whatever they did have. Collections were taken up, especially in the churches. Asa's father made a special appeal at his Sunday service, and the money came pouring in, even though the people had little enough for themselves.

Asa helped his father in this time of trouble and led the church hymns with his beautiful baritone voice, a voice that people kept on saying he "should do something with."

Hard as it was for him, the Reverend James Randolph finally had to admit that his elder son was not naturally cut out for the ministry. He was more than smart enough, but he was very quiet. James, Jr., kept most of his thoughts to himself. His greatest delight was in thinking about the mysteries of mathematics and the sciences. As for the way he got along with other people, he was neither unfriendly nor very sociable.

Asa, on the other hand, was a "people's man," a man interested in everything having to do with his neighbors and his community. Sometimes the minister felt very hopeful about Asa, and sometimes he felt sad, especially when he got the feeling that neither of the boys was as religious as a minister's son should be.

These were times when everybody was talking about Booker T. Washington, the most admired black man in the United States. He had accomplished what no other African American had done or even thought possible.

Washington had started out as a slave. In 1865, all slaves gained their freedom. Soon he had to leave school to work in the salt furnaces and coal mines. He was nine years of age. Washington was determined to become educated. He worked as a janitor at the Hampton Normal and Agricultural Institute in Virginia in order to go to school there. He became a teacher and

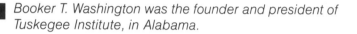 Booker T. Washington was the founder and president of Tuskegee Institute, in Alabama.

went on to become head of the Tuskegee Normal and Industrial School, which was the most famous school for black students in the country in the period following Reconstruction. Many ex-slave farm laborers went there to learn crafts and industrial skills. Washington taught: Don't get the white man angry at you, and make the most of what he allows you. Don't get involved in politics. Don't try to put yourself on the white man's level. And if you play the game according to the white man's rules, you can do all right for yourself. But if you try to fight the white man, he will crush you.

Booker T. Washington was the author of 12 books. His autobiography, *Up from Slavery*, was published in 1901. He was richly rewarded by the whites, who had the real power in the country. They always insisted that his seal of approval be put on all blacks and black organizations applying for government support. If Booker T. said no, then they wouldn't get the backing of rich and powerful whites.

Asa was enraged by Washington's message to "get along" with the system of racism. He was enraged that Washington agreed with the racists that black people should "stay in their place."

Asa often talked about these feelings with his family. He agreed with his father that anger and hatred, if they are not kept under control, can sometimes do more harm than good. But he believed his people had to fight back or they would be oppressed forever. Asa's father did not argue with him, but he always closed their discussions by advising his son that much was in God's hands and that everything, even the black people's suffering, was part of God's plan.

Standing against Booker T. Washington was W.E.B. Du Bois, whose book of essays, *The Souls of Black Folk*, appeared in 1903. Asa read it over and over again. He enjoyed the book for its beautiful writing, but most of all he read it to learn all the ways of his people's suffering. He shared with Du Bois the hurt and wonder at the racists' ability to cause so much suffering, to act so brutally. It thrilled Asa when Du Bois pointed out that the most humble black people were really heroes and people of great dignity. Du Bois gave people hope and made them feel proud. Unlike Washington, Du Bois called on his people to fight for full equality, to fight every injustice against African Americans.

Jacksonville had been slower than other parts of the South in creating a system of segregation. But, by the early 1900s, it was becoming just like the rest of the South. The public parks were forbidden to blacks, as well as other places where black people used to enjoy themselves. Many stores made black people wait until all the white customers had been served. They wouldn't let them try on clothes as white people did. Jobs were closed to blacks. It didn't matter how smart or how much skill the black job seekers had. Voting became more and more difficult.

Asa felt frustrated. He felt he had so much to give, so many talents, but he could find no opportunity to develop them. He went from collecting insurance money to putting down railroad tracks and then to shoveling coal. The more he felt himself growing mentally, the more depressed he became. Finally, he could bear it no longer.

A friend of his was taking a job as a kitchen helper on board a boat heading North, and he told Asa there was another opening. The work was dirty, hot, and tiring. But it would only be for a few days and it would get them to New York. Then Asa could breathe a little freer. New York would be a place where he could study, for there was that great City College of New York. Because many others had found opportunities there, Asa felt that with his gifts, New York would be just the place where he could make his mark.

It was just as Shakespeare wrote:

> To thine own self be true,
> And it must follow, as the night the day,
> Thou canst not then be false to any man.

That boat headed north, and Asa was on it.

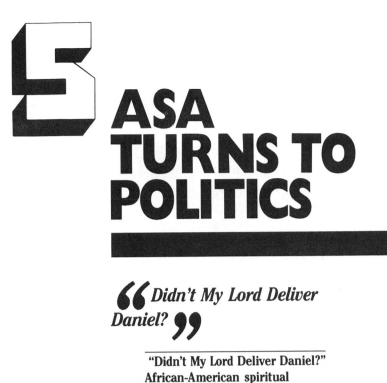

5 ASA TURNS TO POLITICS

❝ *Didn't My Lord Deliver Daniel?* ❞

"Didn't My Lord Deliver Daniel?"
African-American spiritual

W ith a slight nip of winter still in the air, spring settled restlessly over the long rows of stately brownstone houses stretching all the way across 135th Street from the Harlem River on the easternmost edge to the towering heights of Morningside Park. Above those heights stood the stone structures of the City College of New York, structures that Asa now entered every day as a student.

It was quite a sight, this Harlem of 1911. Black people from all over the South were streaming in there and settling in. The streets were teeming with life, with noise, with music, with the sounds of laughter and the sounds of quarrels. Asa, strolling up and down the streets, didn't want to miss a thing, celebrating a new life and his 22nd birthday at the same time.

Great men of color lived in Harlem, and in particular the two brothers Rosamond and James Weldon Johnson. They were famous for their story writing and their music. But to Asa, their greatest accomplishment was the writing of what was called the Negro national anthem.

> Lift every voice and sing
> 'Til earth and heaven ring
> Ring with the harmonies of liberty

Asa found himself walking to the beat of the anthem, all dressed up in his smart derby hat and fine brown chesterfield coat, which had been sewn by his mother. He studied the people crowding the streets and loved the great variety in the shades of their skin and the ways in which they dressed.

It was a sharp climb up to the college, but he fairly bounced up the steps every evening for his classes in history, economics, and other subjects that were called the social sciences. Asa's mind was like a sponge. But it was a challenging mind, too. Asa was determined to make up his own mind and not just to take the word of the professors. He dared to think thoughts that others considered dangerous.

Asa became attracted to the writings of Karl Marx, the father of communism. It was a time when many workers were becoming interested in Marx, and quite a few of the most educated people, too. Marx was against the great owners of property and took the side of the working people. It seemed to some people that the wealthy had taken over the country and had paid off the politicians to do whatever the wealthy people wanted. In the meantime, the working people had no say. While they themselves remained desperately poor, their labor made others very rich. This was how Asa saw things. He believed that the working people were being taken advantage of—all working people, but especially the African-American people. And he decided

A. Philip Randolph during his college years. He attended the City College of New York.

that the reason for all this was "the system," the economic and political system.

Asa became a socialist. There were all kinds of socialists who believed in different things. But for Asa, socialism meant the working people taking charge of their lives and living in dignity, having enough to eat and a decent home to live in. It meant having the right to a good education. It meant an end to racism.

Asa became very interested in labor unions. He saw that when working people did not have unions, they could not stand up to their bosses and could not earn enough to feed their families. But with a union they could make things better. Such an organization would be made up of workers with the same kind of job who agreed to pull together to fight for better pay and better treatment. If the workers had a union, and the boss would not agree to pay them what they thought was fair, the workers could go out on strike. That meant they would all stop work at the same time. In this way, the boss could not keep his business open and would not be able to make money, either.

Now that Asa had "seen the light," he was sure that he would have no trouble showing others the way. But when he began to speak in churches about his socialist ideas, he found that people were cold to his message. He was told that the Lord would set things right, that one should have faith. He was told about the power of prayer. As the son of a minister, he knew these arguments. But even his father had grabbed a gun when a stand had to be taken.

In addition to trying to spread the word of socialism, Asa spent a lot of time enjoying the theater. His love for the theater burned as bright as ever. He acted in a number of plays put on by small groups and had many friends who were actors and writers. He thought he could become famous as an actor, and he was encouraged by the way people responded to him, whether he was acting or reading from the works of such great black poets as Claude McKay, Paul Laurence Dunbar, and Langston Hughes.

But he himself was held spellbound when he stood and listened to the street-corner speakers all up and down 135th Street. They really stirred up the crowds as they called attention to the oppression of black people and called upon them to stand up for their freedom.

Bright as Asa was, the only job he could get to support himself while he went to school at night was as a cleaner at the Consolidated Edison Company. That company provided electricity for the city. That was about all blacks could expect to get: the poorest-paying, dirtiest, most dangerous jobs that whites didn't want. For black people, a job was good if it was steady. Many times they would find work for a few days or a few months and then be let go. Somehow they had to find a way to keep going until they picked up their next job. Asa saw others as well educated as he who were sweeping floors or washing windows.

When Asa tried to get some of the black people together at his company to better their conditions, he found they were too frightened to stand up for themselves. After a while, seeing it was useless, he gave up and quit his job.

Asa managed to get work as a waiter on a steamboat, the *Paul Revere*, that sailed from New York to Boston. He had to lie about his experience because he had never done this kind of work before. Things were going fairly well until one of the people he was serving asked for a "littleneck." What in the world was a littleneck, Asa asked himself, not knowing that it was a kind of clam. What a commotion there was when Asa proceeded to bring out a juicy sirloin steak! Asa managed to talk the headwaiter out of firing him, and he worked for the rest of the trip.

But there was no way Asa could talk himself out of being fired when it was found out that he had been trying to organize the waiters and the kitchen workers to protest the terrible conditions in the "glory hole." The glory hole was a tiny living area, smelly and full of rats. There was only one small light bulb, and it was too dim to read by. Here the workers slept, drank, cursed, and gambled. They often got into fights with one another out of anger at the way they were forced to live.

Rather than try to satisfy the workers, the shipowner decided it was easier to throw Asa, the "trouble-maker," off the ship.

When Asa told the story to his fellow members of a group he

had just joined called the New York Independent Political Council, they slapped him on the back. For they, too, wanted to fight for change. The members of the council spent much of their time speaking to groups of people and passing out articles and pamphlets they had written. They believed that the politicians, the mayors, the governors, and even the president were just helping out their rich friends, while poor people had no one to turn to. Members of the council wanted people to learn about and understand this political viewpoint.

Asa threw himself into these activities with enthusiasm. Later on, when thinking back upon those times, he wrote: "We were having a great time. We didn't think of the future of establishing a home, getting ahead, or things of that sort. Those things weren't as important as creating unrest among the Negroes."

Asa's great ability on the stage and his power as a speaker when talking to groups about politics came to the attention of a man who was the head of a theater company. Asa was asked to join his company. This was to be an important turning point in his life. It was something Asa had always dreamed of. Now that dream was about to become reality.

But Asa wanted his parents' blessing. He was not sure how they would react. He knew they had not given up on their hope for him to become a preacher. And he knew that to many people back home acting on the stage seemed more like playing than serious work. Would he be able to convince his parents that this was a life worthy of a son of theirs?

He wrote home and waited nervously for their reply. It was a sad day for Asa when it came. His parents told him they would never approve of such foolishness.

Asa was a grown man. He could have disobeyed his parents. But he loved them and did not want to hurt them. He put his dreams aside and decided to give himself completely to the freedom struggle, to the workers' struggle, to the struggle of the African-American people.

6 FINDING LOVE

> ** _In that great gettin' up morning!_ **

"Great Gettin' Up Morning,"
African-American spiritual

The sweet clean smells of hair perfume floated down the long hallway of the building, making Asa's nose tingle. He saw women going in and coming out of the far door, most often smiling when they left. It was no wonder, Asa thought, for they came out with their hair newly pressed, curled, and waved. It seemed like magic.

It was not long before Asa met the woman who was creating the hair styles. She was a little older than Asa, a graduate of Howard University, a smart dresser, and delightful to look at.

Asa Philip Randolph was quite suddenly taken by this lovely and sparkling young woman, Lucille Campbell Green. It was hard for him to think up selling ideas at his job for Earnest J. Welcome's Brotherhood of Labor Employment Agency anymore. He had to write advertisements that would excite thousands of blacks to move North to New York and seek work and training with Welcome. This he always did with great success, but now it was hard to think about anything else but her. As if things were not almost perfect, it turned out that Lucille was also a socialist who was truly concerned about the welfare of her people.

Lucille had given up teaching to go to work for Madame C.J. Walker, a black woman who had become a millionaire by making and selling hair products for black people. Thanks to her, black people could now straighten, curl, or manage their naturally kinky hair, hair they were ashamed of. They could have hundreds of different styles and, most important, make their hair look like white people's. Madame Walker had started beauty schools in many cities, and Lucille Green had become one of her first graduates.

Asa, who had kept his head in his books and studies, was known not to have paid too much attention to the opposite sex in the past. But now he was not to be stopped in his pursuit of Lucille. Lucille quickly fell in love with him.

Asa and Lucille had so much in common. They both would give their last dollar to someone in need. Lucille became active in a small group called Ye Friends of Shakespeare, sharing a love of theater with Asa. She was active in the Harlem Fresh Air Fund, which gave poor children a little holiday in the country that their parents could not afford to pay for.

Lucille was taken with Asa's fine good looks, his elegant manner, and his impressive way of speaking. She was attracted to his devotion to the cause of their people. And she was amazed at his great intelligence. It seemed to her that he had read just about every book that was ever written. Lucille saw that Asa did not care very much about money, that he was too busy working for justice to notice that he didn't have a lot of things that made life easier. Since she had a good profession and was very generous, she didn't mind at all paying for some of the things Asa needed.

They called each other "Buddy," a name that seemed to express how really close they were to each other. It seemed to mean more to them than the usual "darling" or "honey."

But although Lucille was a serious woman, she also loved to have a good time. She loved going to parties, and Madame Walker invited her to many. Some parties she held in her grand town house on 136th Street, and some she held outside the city, in the fancy neighborhoods of Westchester County.

Asa and Lucille agreed to get married. For Lucille, this was her second marriage. Her first husband had died when he was still a young man.

Lucille moved in fashionable circles. She was a member of St. Philip's Episcopal Church in Harlem, which had one of the richest congregations of black people in the country. It was considered a great honor to be a member of that church. One was immediately thought of as belonging to the "better element of Colored people."

Asa, on the other hand, never went to dances or parties. Nor did he hang around people of wealth. One of the few times Asa and Lucille had an argument, it had to do with the wedding plans. Asa did not like St. Philip's or the way most of its members acted, pretending to be better than most black working people. Also, he had moved further and further away from religion and was angry at what he felt was the unwillingness of the church to take a stand on the things that were really weighing people down.

Lucille was afraid that the church people, many of whom were her friends, would turn their backs on her. She insisted they marry in St. Philip's, and Asa finally gave in. The wedding, in 1914, went smoothly, even though the minister who joined them together was none too pleased with Asa's well-known socialist views.

As a honeymoon trip, Asa took his bride on an open streetcar ride down to the tip of Manhattan and back. It may not have been a cruise on a luxury ship, but it was fun anyway. It was certainly better to Lucille than spending their honeymoon attending a Socialist party meeting. For Asa could very well have asked her to do that instead. But she understood that he was dedicated to working for a better life for his people and that that was the most important thing in his life.

After they were married, Lucille continued to go to the parties given by Mrs. Walker, and of course Asa continued to stay away from them.

It was at one of those parties that Mrs. Walker introduced Lucille to a very clever, fast-talking man by the name of Chandler Owen. Short, full of energy, he would bounce around the room picking arguments with anyone he could find willing to take him on, especially about politics. Lucille noticed how he always got the better of his opponents. Although he was a kind man, he had a very sharp tongue. The trouble was he couldn't see that much wrong with the way things were. Lucille wondered whether he got his ideas from Columbia University, where he was studying at the time. She also wondered what kind of sparks would fly if she introduced Chandler to Asa.

Finally, Lucille did introduce Owen to her husband, and they hit it off right away. They would remain friends for the rest of their lives. Though they liked each other, in the beginning they argued all the time about their different political ideas. But soon, Owen was won over to Randolph's socialist policies. Both Owen and Randolph were full-time students. Both of them gave up their jobs so they could learn the secrets of society. They needed to find out much more about why it was, for example, that people lived the way they did. They wanted to know why it was that some people had power while most others had none at all. They wanted to know why nations were always going to war. And they wanted to know, above all, what was the way out of the misery of the black people of America.

Owen Chandler. He and A. Philip Randolph published the African-American magazine the Messenger.

Both Owen and Randolph plunged into socialist activities and studied socialist writings. They came to a clearer understanding of what socialism really was. They learned that socialism meant that the working people would own all the factories, the coal and oil, the land, and the buildings. They learned that people would not have to work for bosses who grew rich from working people's labor. They found out that socialism also meant that landlords would not be taking rents from people anymore, that the banks would be taken over by the people.

Randolph and Owen never missed going to hear Eugene

Debs, when he came to New York. They considered him the greatest man in the Socialist party. Randolph said, "I had not met a white man with such spiritual character, such a great and warm feeling for the human vision of socialism." They listened to other socialist speakers, as well. But they were often disappointed because those speakers did not seem to be paying enough attention to the suffering of black people. When Randolph and Owen questioned them about this, they would say only that the problems of black people would be taken care of only after there was a socialist society. That was indeed a long time to wait.

Randolph and Owen loved to listen to the powerful black socialist Hubert H. Harrison. He drew large crowds as he spoke on the corner of Lenox Avenue and 135th Street.

How had Randolph and Owen managed to keep going without jobs? How had they managed to remain full-time students? It was thanks to Lucille Randolph, whose good earnings were used to support both Randolph and Owen. She was willing to support them because she believed in the importance of what they were doing. Lucille's beauty business made a lot of money. Her services were in demand even by wealthy white women on Park Avenue.

In 1916, Chandler Owen and A. Philip Randolph decided to take an important step together. They had up to that time just agreed with what the Socialist party was saying. Now they decided to join that party. They were sure this step would give them new power. They thought now they would be able to go full speed ahead with their message of freedom and their message to the working people: "Organize!"

7 TURNING TO THE WORKERS

> ## **"** *For the union makes us strong.* **"**
>
> RALPH CHAPLIN,
> "Solidarity Forever"

After a while, Randolph and Owen dropped out of their schools and spent all their time in meetings and speech making. Randolph, being the more gifted, became president of their own organization, the Independent Political Council, while Owen became the executive secretary.

The aim of their organization was to educate the people as to the reasons for their present terrible conditions. Randolph and Owen thought that the politicians, whom the people still believed in, were actually lying to them and helping to keep them down. The way to start solving their problems was to rid themselves of these politicians.

Little by little, they built up a following. More and more people stopped to listen to them as they gave their weeknight talks on the corner of 135th Street and Lenox Avenue. Before long, they had a larger crowd than the famous Hubert Harrison.

Woodrow Wilson, the Democratic party candidate, had been elected president in 1912. The people were shocked at the difference between the promises he had made to black people before the election and how he actually treated them after he became president. He had promised to fight against discrimination. He had promised to see to it that blacks would become full and equal citizens of the United States. But now he brought segregation into the federal government offices in Washington, D.C. Black government workers were fired. Separate water fountains, eating rooms, and toilets were put in for blacks and whites. Members of Congress were calling for segregation in buses and trains, in the army, the navy, at jobs, schools—everywhere.

The Knights of the Ku Klux Klan, the White Camelias, and other violent hate groups were growing stronger throughout the land. The threat of lynching was everywhere, especially in the South. But even in the North, to which blacks were streaming for jobs or to escape southern terror, there were many attacks on blacks and huge antiblack riots.

Randolph talked to his people about these things. For him, the only way to fight all this was for black workers to get together, for as individuals they could do nothing. An important first step would be to join unions and fight the employers, for unions could become strong enough to stand up to the bosses, stand up to the mobs, and stand up to the government.

But the trouble was that whites wouldn't let blacks join unions. As a matter of fact, most unions of the day only took care of a small group of men who had skills and who were paid better than the average worker. As far as blacks were concerned, most unions couldn't have cared less about them—or about foreign-born whites and women.

So Randolph and Owen decided that if the whites were not going to let blacks into their unions, then the only thing left to do was to set up their own unions.

They began by trying to get a union started among the black men who ran the elevators. This was one of the few jobs that black men were allowed to have. Randolph and Owen walked from building to building, talking with the workers. In a matter of only a few weeks, they had signed up about 600 members. They were going to demand $18 a week in pay, which was still low but in that day it was possible to live on that amount of money. They were also asking to work no more than 8 hours a day. At that time, workers put in 10 and even 12 hours a day. In order to win these things, the workers would have to go out on strike. They would all have to agree to refuse to work. But the workers were too frightened to take that step. They feared they would lose their jobs. So the effort to help the elevator operators failed.

Hearing about Randolph's and Owen's work with the elevator men, the head of a group of restaurant waiters offered them a large space for the Independent Political Council if in return they would help put out a newspaper for the waiters. Randolph and Owen jumped at the chance. The paper appeared for almost a year with their help. It was called the *Hotel Messenger.* It was then that Randolph decided to use the name A. Philip Randolph when he signed his articles. People who knew him very well called him Phil. Most people called him Mr. Randolph.

Randolph wrote not only about the conditions of the waiters, but he wrote on other subjects as well. Their office became a favorite meeting place for many of those who were seeking to change society.

In April 1917, President Wilson declared war against Germany. "The world must be made safe for democracy. . . . We have no selfish ends to serve. . . . We are but one of the champions of the rights of mankind," said Wilson. He was trying to explain to people why he had broken his promise to keep the United

United States out of World War I. The war had broken out in Europe, where the fighting had already been going on for almost three years. To many black people, his words were received with bitterness indeed, for while Wilson was going to war for democracy thousands of miles away, black people were suffering from a lack of rights at home.

In the meantime, Randolph's and Owen's honesty cost them their jobs on the newspaper. They learned that the headwaiters in the union had been cheating. They had been demanding large amounts of money from the assistant waiters who helped them in waiting on tables. They had no right to this money. Randolph and Owen printed a story about it in the union newspaper, publicly revealing this dirty practice. Here was an example of people who themselves were badly treated now turning on those below them. The assistant waiters had been afraid to talk about it. The headwaiters were outraged at having all this printed in their own union paper. Randolph and Owen were immediately fired.

Many alarming things were happening to black people around the country. In September 1917, thirteen black soldiers were hanged in Houston, Texas, and 41 were sentenced to life imprisonment after a race riot. The blacks were unjustly blamed for the riot. To protest that injustice, 15,000 African Americans marched down Fifth Avenue in New York City. Randolph was among them, carrying a sign that said, "Mr. President, why not make America safe for democracy?"

In 1917, in East St. Louis, Illinois, at least 40 blacks were killed, and hundreds more were injured in a race riot. White mobs went wild, frustrated at their own poor conditions and believing that blacks were taking jobs and housing away from them. The whites would not let black workers join their unions. But if the whites went out on strike and black workers took their places in the factories, the whites called them scabs and attacked them.

In the meantime, World War I was raging in Europe. Men

The Silent March of 1917 down New York's Fifth Avenue protested lynchings and segregation.

were being drafted every day, including black men. But the black soldiers were put in all-black units, often to do servant work. Many times they were not allowed to have arms with which to fight in case of battle. Lies were spread in Europe. The people there were told that they should not mix with black soldiers. The story was even spread that black men had tails!

Randolph spoke before large crowds in Harlem and around the country. He explained to the people what was going on and asked them to stand up for their rights.

Having lost the newspaper of the waiters' union, in 1917 Randolph decided to start a magazine. It was named the *Messenger.* For the truth had to be spread as far as possible and reach as many people as possible. Owen worked with him and stood by him.

In November, in the very first issue, the *Messenger* hurled its challenge. Randolph and Owen were not going to hide what they stood for.

They said that capitalism was a way of life in which a small group of people made money from the work of others. Socialism would not allow this. According to them, under socialism, the people would be working for the benefit of all.

They said that the rich were keeping white and black workers fighting each other, instead of opposing the rich. This must stop. The workers must start a revolution. They must become the rulers; that is, they must control the government and all the riches of the country.

It was dangerous enough for whites to talk like this. But for blacks, it could be suicidal.

A. Philip Randolph at that moment finally felt free. He could speak about the subjects that meant the most to him—and he could do it without biting his tongue. He could tell what he believed to be the truth about the poverty and joblessness, the lynchings, and the lack of rights of his people. He knew the people were looking for leadership. He felt that through his magazine the people would get that leadership.

8 THE MESSENGER

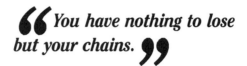

> **" You have nothing to lose but your chains. "**

KARL MARX,
Communist Manifesto

Soon, Randolph's magazine was the talk of black New York, and some of white New York, as well. Printed beneath its title was: "The Only Radical Negro Magazine in America."

The tone of the magazine was hard anger. There was no beating around the bush. The writing was direct and it was exciting.

The *Messenger* waged a fierce battle against the war and urged black people not to fight, not to enlist, and not to let themselves be drafted. The war was to be waged at home, as far as Ran-

The Messenger

Published monthly by The Messenger Publishing Co.,
513 Lenox Ave., New York City

A. PHILIP RANDOLPH,
President.

CHANDLER OWEN,
Secretary-Treasurer.

——— : o : ———

CONTENTS

Entered as second class mail matter at New York Post Office, N. Y., March, 1917,
under the act of March 5, 1879.

dolph was concerned. According to the *Messenger*, it was ridiculous for blacks to fight "to make the world safe for democracy" when there was no democracy for them in the United States. Not only that, but the war had been started because countries like England, France, and Germany were fighting among themselves to see who would rule over the darker peoples of Africa and Asia. The Europeans had conquered the native populations of Africa and Asia and set up colonies. They forced the Africans and Asians to work for them for practically nothing. They were not fighting about democracy. They were fighting over the riches they could obtain from the colonies' natural wealth—minerals, such as gold and oil, and agricultural products like cocoa and cotton. They were fighting about cheap labor. African Americans had no business becoming a part of this, said the *Messenger*.

Moreover, Randolph did not believe in violence. He was a pacifist, someone who is morally opposed to all wars.

The *Messenger* was speaking out against the war at a time when thousands of people who opposed the war were being arrested. Anybody who spoke against the war was called a traitor or a German spy.

The most powerful organization of black people in the country at the time was the National Association for the Advancement of Colored People (NAACP). Its view about the war was different from Randolph's. The NAACP felt that the war would give black people a chance to prove their courage and their abilities, and that as a result, they would be given their rights after the war. So it urged black people to serve loyally in the armed forces.

The *Messenger* had bitter words for this view. It reported with anger the 1917 killing of black soldiers in Texas and the riots in East St. Louis. It spoke out in favor of women having the right to vote, for it was not until three years later, in 1920, that women finally won that right. The *Messenger* spoke up for the Irish who were battling for national freedom against the British. It demanded that those who were growing rich through the war pay for it. For the *Messenger*, there was a quick way to end the war: "...see to it that the government confiscates [takes] all profits made out of the war to carry on the war. Let the government take 100 percent and peace will come...."

Randolph was disgusted by the way ministers said one thing in church and then did another outside the church. To make the point, he printed a poem by Walter Everett Hawkins, which began:

> Too much talk of heaven
> Too much talk of golden streets
> When one can't be sympathetic
> When needy neighbors meet.

Randolph also published the works of such great black poets as Countee Cullen, Langston Hughes, Claude McKay, and Wallace Thurman.

When the Russian Revolution broke out in 1917, the *Messenger* cheered. For to Randolph, this was a case of the poor freeing themselves from the rich.

When Morris Hillquit ran for mayor of New York as the Socialist party candidate, Randolph and Owen were asked to get black people to vote for Hillquit. They did, and Hillquit got 25 percent of the Harlem vote. This was an amazing figure. For black people at that time almost always voted for the Republican party, the party that they felt had freed them from slavery and had been their friend for many years.

Because of the loud opposition to the war, the offices of the *Messenger* were broken into by the federal government. Papers were thrown all about. The offices were left in a shambles.

The Congress of the United States had just passed the Espionage Act in June 1917. This act allowed the government to prevent people from writing whatever they wanted to about the war. Then Congress passed another law making it a crime to tell people not to go into the armed forces. Eugene Debs and many other socialists had already been sentenced to jail for this—in fact, Debs got 10 years.

True, the raiding of the offices of the *Messenger* had caused fear, but it would not stop Randolph and Owen. They arranged for a public-speaking tour of several large cities "to speak against the war and to get Colored people interested in the socialist movement."

On August 4, Randolph and Owen were to speak before a large meeting in Cleveland, Ohio. Just as Randolph was about to begin his talk, a government agent jumped onto the stage, carrying a copy of the July issue of the *Messenger*. That issue, like all the others, had told people not to support the war. This violated the Espionage Act, the government said. Randolph and Owen were arrested and immediately taken to prison.

Randolph would remember his trial with amusement. The judge had been amazed when he read what was published in the *Messenger*. He looked at Randolph and then at Owen. They seemed like innocent boys to him. He couldn't believe they were capable of writing that "red hot stuff." Nor could he believe that blacks could write so intelligently. In his mind, they were not responsible for the *Messenger*. It had to be the dangerous white socialists.

Turning to the lawyer for Randolph and Owen, the judge said, "I don't think we are going to have a trial. I am going to release these boys in your custody, and I want you to see to it that they return to their parents' homes."

The *Messenger* was now the talk of the nation.

MARCUS GARVEY

> **❝ Ethiopia shall stretch forth her hand. ❞**
>
> ───────────────
> **African-American folk saying**

T he few days spent in that dark and gloomy jail frightened and angered A. Philip Randolph and Chandler Owen. However, it was the kind of experience that made them even stronger. After being released, they continued moving around the country, sharing their thoughts with eager audiences.

"The gospel of *obey* and *trust* has been replaced by one of *rebel* and *demand*," they thundered. Their audiences cheered, but most people were afraid to stick their necks out and oppose the government, as Randolph and Owen were doing.

There were nearly 400,000 black soldiers serving in the U.S.

military. More than 50,000 of them were sent overseas. It was the black soldiers of the 368th Infantry Regiment that had played a big role in turning the tide of battle when the French army was losing. In desperation, the French finally turned to the 368th, gave them guns and ammunition, and the French were saved. When a white-owned paper in the Midwest received the news of this great feat, its only comment was that the black troops should be honored with a truckload of watermelon. (Many whites made fun of what they thought was blacks' special love for this fruit.)

Randolph and Owen finished their speaking tour and came back to New York only to find that their offices had been broken into again. The government in Washington would not give them any peace. The Justice Department called them "the most dangerous Negroes in America."

In the middle of the summer, Owen was called into the army, and two months later, Randolph was called up, too. However, just two days before Randolph was to report to the army, the fighting in Europe came to an end. The world war was over.

Now Randolph was in great demand. Thousands wanted to hear his socialist message. It was just about that time that a young man from Jamaica, an island in the Caribbean Sea, approached him. Randolph had noticed him many times hanging around the street corner where Randolph often spoke. This short, round man, with an extremely proud manner, wanted Randolph to speak with his followers at the Palace Casino on West 135th Street. That man, who was to become the leader of the most powerful movement of black people of his time, was Marcus Garvey.

Randolph felt that he had a lot in common with Garvey—the same kind of pride, the same faith in the future of his people. He agreed to help Garvey make the meeting a success. He would not only speak at the meeting, but he would also spread the word about it and ask people to come.

The day of the meeting arrived. It was called by one of Garvey's organizations, the International League of Darker Peoples. The war had come to an end and peace terms were being discussed in Europe. So the meeting was called to demand that Europe's African colonies be set free.

It was necessary to send someone over to the peace conference in Europe who could speak for Africa. Who should that person be? All eyes turned to Randolph. There was no question about it. Ida Wells Barnett was chosen, too. She was a fearless newspaper reporter from Tennessee who had fled from southern terror to New York. Money was collected from the gathering to send them to France.

But the U.S. government had other ideas. It would be too embarrassing for them and the European nations to let Randolph speak. Several European nations had empires controlling millions of Africans and Asians. The government would not give him a passport, so Randolph could not leave the country.

Randolph once again plunged into the battle for his people at home. More than ever, he was convinced of the need to develop strong unions. He tried to organize the laundry workers, restaurant workers, and the workers who made clothes. He passed out literature urging them to join. He spent endless hours talking to workers, one at a time. But all his attempts to form unions failed. The workers were too afraid. They knew they could be easily replaced by their bosses. There were so many people out of work who would jump at the chance to take away someone else's job.

The period between 1917 and 1919 was a terrible one for blacks. Nearly 400,000 black soldiers had served in the military. Many other blacks had worked in war industries. Yet once the war was over, they were discriminated against even more. Hundreds of blacks, including the soldiers and workers, were beaten, imprisoned, and lynched. In the last half of 1919, there were 25 race riots in cities in the North and South. Historians say the cause was the whites' fears of economic competition from black workers.

By 1920, Marcus Garvey's fame was spreading. Hundreds of thousands joined his organization called the Universal Negro Improvement Association. At a time when whites in the United States seemed to be filled with hatred against blacks, Garvey spoke about the need for black people to have their own land. He told them that they should no longer depend on white people. He said they should all put their money together and build great black businesses. He painted a picture of black people owning big factories in cities in the United States, Central America, the Caribbean, Africa—everywhere black people were to be found.

Garvey felt it was foolish for blacks to try to fight for their rights in the United States because whites would never give up their superior position and their rule.

But Randolph did not agree. He felt that Garvey was leading the black people in the wrong direction. Randolph maintained that the only way for black people to win their freedom was by staying and fighting for a new life in the United States. He saw that black-owned factories would be a good thing only for the few blacks who were rich enough to buy them. But black working people would not be any better off because the factories would never belong to them.

Still, Garvey's power and influence kept growing stronger. He began a shipping line called the Black Star Line. He was going to buy a whole fleet of ships that would carry black people home to Africa to start a new life. He started a fighting group called the African Legion to protect the people when they returned to Africa. And he formed a special group of black nurses to care for them.

In August 1920, the largest of all the Garvey meetings took place in Madison Square Garden in New York City. Black people came from all over the world. It was reported that 25,000 people filled the hall.

Garvey declared himself "Provisional President of Africa." When he came out on stage and told his audience that the Europeans who had enslaved Africa would be overthrown, the crowd went wild. The way he put it was that "Ethiopia would stretch forth her wings and take control."

But soon, stories began to spread that Garvey was becoming rich from the money people were sending him to buy ships. Randolph heard these stories, but he knew that whites would say anything to make Garvey look bad.

Randolph also heard that Garvey had met with leaders of the Ku Klux Klan. This was a group that had brought much terror and death to black people, especially through lynchings. It turned out to be true that Garvey and the Klan had come to an agreement that the races should remain separated. This was something that Randolph could not accept.

Randolph and Owen called for all black leaders to defeat Garvey and what he stood for. The fight was on for the minds and ears of black people. Which course would they take? Would they follow Garvey and try to establish a separate nation or would they fight for their rights within the United States? Much was at stake. Sometimes the argument got so bitter that members of different groups got into fistfights. Randolph became worried about his safety. He had many enemies. Not only were the followers of Garvey after him, but white racists wanted to get him, too.

One day, a package came to the *Messenger* office with the return address on it marked "From a Friend." It had been mailed from New Orleans. As Randolph started to open it, a white powder fell out. Fearing the powder was part of a bomb that had been planted in the package, he called the police. The police came and opened it. Inside they discovered a human hand! Was this a warning that somebody was going to cut off Randolph's hand or kill him? It was a time when Randolph received many death threats. But fear could not keep A. Philip Randolph from doing what he thought was right.

These were difficult days for Randolph, but there were some bright moments, too. His brother, James William, Jr., came to live with him and to attend the City College of New York. Owen's brother, too, came from South Carolina to New York to work as a tailor. He had a tailor shop at home, but the people in his community were too poor to be able to pay him for his services. Owen thought that since there were some friendly whites in the needle trade unions in New York, they would be able to find him a job.

James, Jr.'s coming brought great joy to Randolph. Even though they had lived apart for many years, they still felt as close as when they were boys growing up together. James was a man who kept to himself, but he had a powerful mind, and although politics was not as important to him as it was to his brother, they still found many things to talk about together.

The *Messenger* was in deep trouble. On the one hand, the government was creating many problems for it. Agents from Washington would burst into its offices, take away important papers, and threaten to close it down. On the other hand, great numbers of black people were caught up with Garvey and his message. They were no longer interested in what Randolph had to say.

But then everything fell apart for Marcus Garvey. The government arrested him for swindling the people, for getting money from them with false promises. Some said the charges against Garvey were false. They said it was a government trick to get rid of him because white people were afraid of him. At any rate, the government sent Garvey back to Jamaica. With Garvey gone, people turned away from his ideas as time went on. When he died in London, he was almost a forgotten man.

Troubles for the Randolph family now kept piling up. Lucille's beauty business, which at one time had been very profitable, was now earning very little money. Many of her customers stopped going to her shop because they were afraid to be seen with the wife of a man they believed to be a dangerous radical.

Then Randolph's long and warm association with his friend Owen came to an end. Owen's brother could not find work in New York, and the friendly whites whom Owen had counted on to help did not really try hard enough, or so it seemed to Owen. Poverty stricken, his brother had become ill and died.

Marcus Garvey (left) on board the S.S. Saramacca before his deportation from New Orleans in 1927.

Owen was enraged at what he felt was the betrayal of his white fellow socialists. He thought they only pretended to care about blacks. He quit the Socialist party and moved to Chicago.

Finally came the saddest of all Randolph's misfortunes. His father died. He and his father had been extremely close. He had indeed disappointed his father by not becoming a minister. James Randolph had been troubled by the terrible things that were said about his son's political activities. But his father had always respected what his son was trying to accomplish. Although they had not always agreed on everything, Randolph respected his father's fighting spirit. He felt his father was a truly decent, strong, and honest human being.

Upon his father's death, Randolph's mother moved to New York to be with her two sons. Randolph, too, was having second thoughts about the Socialist party. Its members seemed to be whites first and socialists second. The Socialist party paid little attention to the needs of blacks. Its beautiful words about equality were only on paper, not put into practice. There were some exceptions, like Eugene Debs, but they were pitifully few.

Randolph, too, quit the party. He had had such high hopes for it at one time. Now those hopes were dead.

10 THE PORTERS ASK FOR HELP

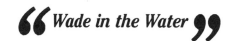
" *Wade in the Water* **"**

"Wade in the Water,"
African-American
spiritual

Asa Philip Randolph sat thinking over the situation in his office at 2311 Seventh Avenue in New York City, thumbing through old issues of the *Messenger* and puzzling over what he was to do with his life now. He had tried to organize his people and failed. He had tried to educate his people and failed. He had to face the bitter truth. The language of the *Messenger* was for educated readers, while his people were mostly uneducated, and in many cases unable to read or write.

The *Messenger* was read by people who already agreed with him. Although many outstanding leaders and thinkers had praised the magazine, it was not for them that it had been published. No, his magazine was a failure, and it had lost a lot of money. Lack of money was something that now pressed hard on Randolph's life. His wife could no longer support him. He had to face reality.

So the idea came to Randolph to put out a new newspaper, one that expressed many different points of view, one that would appeal to a wider audience, not just the handful of socialists that the *Messenger* had reached up to then.

Randolph managed to get a number of very good writers to contribute to the paper. George Schuyler began writing for it. Later, he would become one of the most famous African-American newspaper writers in the country. The paper was called *The Black Worker.* Owen helped out, too, sending articles from Chicago and selling ads for the paper whenever he could. In the middle of the work involved in trying to get the *Messenger* free of debt, a meeting took place that changed the entire course of Randolph's life.

One day in June 1925, as he was setting out for his office and had reached West 135th Street, Randolph was stopped by a tall, very well-dressed black man. He introduced himself as Ashley L. Totten. He told Randolph that he was from St. Croix in the Virgin Islands, but that he had been living in Harlem for a number of years. He said he was working as a Pullman Railroad sleeping-car porter. He wanted Randolph to speak to a group of other sleeping-car porters at a special meeting called to talk about forming a union.

Randolph was surprised. His own past record at organizing unions had not been successful. And some of his ideas frightened people. They were not ready to go as far as he was to change the way things were in the country. But Totten was sure that Randolph was the man for the job. The Pullman porters were in a bad way. When they asked the company for some improvement in their conditions, the company told them that if they didn't like it, they could find other jobs.

Ashley Totten (third from right) shown here with A. Philip Randolph and other leaders of the BSCP.

Totten had read the *Messenger* and knew about Randolph's message to the workers to organize. So did some of the porters. In fact, some of the porters had heard his speeches on the street corners and were convinced that he was the man to lead them. He was a powerful speaker and understood their problems. Best of all, since he did not work for the Pullman Company, he could not be fired for trying to build a union. Not all the porters were happy about working with Randolph, however. Some thought he was "putting on airs" because of his very proper manners and his very correct speech. But the majority of porters were all for him.

Randolph met with four of the porters' leaders and they urged him to take charge of an organizing drive. Randolph told them he was happy that they had so much confidence in him, but he didn't think he could succeed. It was one thing to write articles and to speak on street corners. It was quite another to take on one of the most powerful corporations in the country. He would be glad to take up their cause in the *Messenger.* But to actually lead their struggle—that seemed a wild idea. But Randolph agreed to think about it.

Randolph now made a serious study of the conditions of the Pullman porters, as well as the few women who worked as maids for the company. He was amazed at what he learned. He found out that the average porter had to be on duty 100 hours a week—more than twice as long as other workers. And they were paid only about $15 a week. Even with tips, they were earning much less than other workers on the railroad. Out of their earnings, they had to buy their own meals and the uniforms they were required to wear. Many times, the porters would end up at a station a long way from home and would not be paid for the time it took them to get back home.

The job of the porter was to make up the beds for the train passengers, brush off their clothes, polish shoes, serve meals, and run errands. A porter had to bow and scrape because he depended on a good tip. A single bad word to the company from a rider could mean the end of his job. As bad as the porter's job was, it was considered a good one in the African-American community because most jobs offered to black men were either backbreaking, dirty, dangerous, or not steady. For that reason, many of the brightest and most educated black men took jobs working as porters. To most white men, it was the kind of job that was looked down on. They would be ashamed to take that kind of work.

Randolph began writing a series of articles describing the bad conditions of the porters. When the porters pleaded with him again to take the leadership, Randolph finally agreed.

And so, on the night of August 25, 1925, the Brotherhood of Sleeping Car Porters was started in the hall of the Imperial Lodge of Elks at 160 West 129th Street in New York City. The meeting was described by the *New York Amsterdam News*, the leading black paper in New York, as "the greatest labor mass meeting ever held of, for and by Negro working men."

Pullman Company spies were everywhere. They would come

to meetings or try to listen in on conversations. Then they would tell everything to the company and thus get the workers into trouble. For the company was determined that there would never be a union of porters. Many times in the past, porters were fired if it was thought they were doing work for a union. The company was cruel and the porters were afraid.

In later years, Randolph would describe how that first meeting was run and how he protected the porters from the spies he knew were in the hall.

A. Philip Randolph (fifth from right) at one of the first meetings of the BSCP.

"I told the men," said Randolph, "I didn't want one porter to open his mouth in the meeting." He wanted to make sure the spies would not be able to report the names of people who played a leading role. "So I ran the whole meeting myself. I told them I would now give the invocation [open with a prayer] and I gave it. I told them I was going to sing the Brotherhood's song, 'Hold the Fort,' and I sang it. I told them I was going to make the announcements and introduce guest speakers, and I did. I told them now I was going to make the main speech, and then I did. At the end of the meeting, I moved the vote of thanks, said the benediction [thanked everybody, gave the blessings], and told everyone to go home and not hold any discussions on the street corners."

The Brotherhood was going to demand shorter working hours and higher wages. It was going to speak up for a lot of other things the porters had a right to. Of course, that included a union.

The day after the meeting, 200 porters came to Randolph's office to join the union. The *Messenger* office was now also the main office of the new Brotherhood. Soon, most of the porters in New York had signed up.

The problem was that the porters were scattered all over the country and were constantly moving about. How could they be reached, especially when there was almost no money to spend to hire people to work for the union?

Randolph turned to some white friends and some socialists for help and got $10,000. Randolph was now ready to tour the country and take on the Pullman Company. The odds were against him. The job was not only difficult, but it was dangerous.

Randolph began his trip around the country.

11 ORGANIZING

Randolph was greeted by the windy heat of Chicago in late August 1925. He went immediately to reach out to the Pullman workers. His neat, well-dressed appearance made a strange impression on them, however. He looked more like an English king than a workingman's leader.

A public meeting had been arranged for Randolph at the Metropolitan Community Church by Milton Webster. Webster was a heavyset man with a powerful voice. A former Chicago porter who had been fired for trying to organize a union, Webster was angry and tough. He had taken great pride in his work for over 20 years. He had done his job well, but the company booted him out anyway. He told the porters he was "ready to fight till hell froze over, and then get a pair of skates and fight on the ice," as Robert Turner had said in his *Memories of a Retired Pullman Porter.*

Webster looked Randolph up and down. His first impression was that it had been a mistake to ask him to come out to Chicago. Still, he went on to introduce him to the gathering of porters, and then he walked all the way to the back of the church, as if he wanted to get as far away as possible. But by the time Randolph had got halfway through his speech, Webster was shaking his fist in agreement. When Randolph finished, Webster jumped up from his seat and announced to all who could hear him, "That's our man! Count me in!" Webster's support was very important. The porters regarded him as the most popular man in Chicago, and they would go along with whatever he advised.

Randolph spent two weeks in Chicago, the home of the Pullman Company. He spoke to group after group, repeating over and over again the main point of his talks: A worker was helpless by himself, but when he came together with his fellow workers they could make miracles. The important thing was not to let anyone or anything split them up.

Things were looking good. But then, Perry Howard, a powerful black politician, started attacking the Brotherhood. Howard had a big job in the Republican party. He was an assistant to the attorney general of the United States, the highest law officer in the country. Perry called Randolph and the other Brotherhood leaders Communists, and Communists were thought to be very dangerous people. Perry demanded that Randolph meet him face to face in a debate.

The way Randolph handled himself now could decide the fate of the porters for a long time to come. Randolph agreed to have a debate with Perry. Perry was sure of himself. He thought he could argue so well that Randolph would be left looking foolish.

Milton Webster (third from right) was the first vice president of the BSCP.

The debate was held in the biggest hall in the black section of Chicago. The place was packed. Of course there were many porters in the hall. It didn't take long for Randolph to make Perry really look bad. In fact, the porters got so angry at Perry that they were ready to beat him up. Webster managed to hold off the crowd until the police came in and got Perry out of the auditorium. Webster couldn't stop laughing as he watched Perry and the police hurrying away. Later on, people found out that Perry was getting money from the Pullman Company to try to stop the union.

Randolph became the hero of the day. Porters now rushed to join the Brotherhood. Randolph addressed different meetings of the porters, speaking coolly and calmly. Reeling off fact after fact, he showed the need for a union and won more and more porters over to his side.

On the night of October 18, 1925, at one of the meetings, a man suddenly jumped onto the stage and began to make an exciting speech. He ripped the Pullman Company apart, showing all the dirty ways the company was making life miserable for the workers. Randolph thought he knew the man from somewhere, but just couldn't seem to remember where. The man told his listeners he had been a porter in New York. He had come to Chicago to hear more about the Brotherhood. When the Pullman Company discovered that he was interested in the Brotherhood, he was fired. Then it dawned on Randolph. This was none other than Ashley L. Totten, the man who had first come to Randolph about helping the Brotherhood.

Pacing up and down the stage, Totten put into burning words what all knew to be true. When he finished, the men stood up and cheered. Webster, smiling, turned to Randolph, who was getting ready to leave to make a trip around the country, and said, "Take that man with you." Randolph agreed. Webster was made second in command in Randolph's absence. Wherever Randolph went, Totten was always by his side. Going from city to city, they became known as Randolph the Saint and Totten the Terrible.

The Pullman porters were unlike the workers Randolph had tried to organize in the past. There were many thousands of porters and they all worked for the same company. So if they all stopped working at the same time, it would be very hard for the Pullman Company to find other workers to take their place. This gave the porters a great deal of courage.

There were many heroes among the porters. There were many brave men whose names have not gone down in history books. But the union could never have been organized without them.

There was, for instance, a man named Bradley in St. Louis who was put in charge of organizing in that city. The local company man, A. V. Burr, was tough and mean, a man who boasted about how much fun it was to whip "niggers." But Bradley was as tough as Burr and ready to lay down his life for the union. To organize openly in St. Louis was to face a high risk of being beaten up or even killed. Randolph and Totten tried to talk Bradley out of opening a public Brotherhood office.

They told him that they would try to organize secretly for him. But Bradley wouldn't hear of it. "Ain't nobody can organize St. Louis but me."

When Burr heard about the opening of the office, he set his spies to watch it around the clock. When he heard about some 30 porters that were seen going inside, he had them fired the same day. This was a big blow to the Brotherhood. The porters were now afraid to come to the union office. Bradley was forced to close it, but he turned the trunk of his car into a new office and just went on organizing.

Randolph kept moving, kept winning followers. He inspired the porters in city after city. The effect Randolph had on those to whom he spoke was described by a porter, E. D. Nixon, who years later was to work closely with Dr. Martin Luther King, Jr. Nixon said that when he heard Randolph "It was like a light. [He was the] most eloquent man [forceful speaker] I ever heard.... I never knew the Negro had a right to enjoy freedom like everyone else. When Randolph stood there and talked that day it made a different man out of me. From that day on, I was determined that I was gonna fight for freedom until I was able to get some of it myself."

By the end of 1926, groups of the Brotherhood had been set up in cities all over the country, from New York on the East Coast to Portland and Los Angeles on the West Coast.

Often, Randolph would run out of money, and then the porters would "pass the hat" for his train fare. But sometimes, even then, he couldn't get any money together. At times he didn't have a nickel to his name. When he heard that his mother, Elizabeth, had died in New York, he couldn't get home to the funeral because he had no money. This was a bitter time for Randolph, and he kept the hurt inside him for a long time.

Randolph's travels were hard. There were no days off, no vacations. He began to have dizzy spells. Once he was so tired he had to be carried to bed. But he insisted on going forward.

At first, the officials of the Pullman Company just laughed when they heard that the porters were still trying to start a

The BROTHERHOOD OF SLEEPING CAR PORTERS
STANDS FOR SERVICE NOT SERVITUDE

LIGHTING THE WAY TO OUR RACE'S ECONOMIC INDEPENDENCE

The BSCP used posters to encourage African-American railroad workers to unionize.

union. The company was rich; the porters had no money. The company had powerful politicians behind it. The porters were pretty much on their own. The Pullman Company thought it could easily crush its workers whenever it wanted. As the manager for the Pullman Company in Chicago told a Brotherhood official when he called him into his office to tell him he was being fired: "Remember, this is a white man's country. White people run it, will keep on running it, and the company will never sit down around the same table with Randolph as long as he's black."

But as strong as the company thought it was, it decided to take no chances. It started putting out a newspaper called the *Pullman Porter Messenger.* This paper spread all kinds of lies about Randolph and the union men. In one issue, it said Randolph was preparing to sneak off to Russia with $72,000 of the porters' money. The company hired spies to report to it any worker who showed interest in becoming a union member. The company fired any worker it thought was on the side of the union. It had friends in the newspaper business who were willing to print whatever the company wanted. It had friends in some of the black churches.

The efforts of the company were having an effect. Some of the porters began wavering. Maybe Randolph *was* a crook, just as the newspapers said. Hadn't leaders pretended to be fighting for them in the past, only to steal their hard-earned money and run off somewhere? Wasn't the company really too strong for them? And wasn't the government ready to do whatever the company wanted? Weren't they crazy to think that poor black porters could stand up to such power?

But Randolph insisted that they talk about those doubts. What Randolph did best was to get the workers to see the good in themselves. He could make them feel that they had the right to demand a good life. He had the ability to get the workers to understand just how really strong they were. The men stood together and were ready to do battle.

In May 1926, in the midst of the struggle, a railway labor act was passed in Washington, known as the Watson-Parker Act. This protected the right of railroad workers to organize. This, too, helped the porters feel stronger.

The Pullman Company was determined, but it was faced with men of equal determination. These men were ready to take a chance on losing their jobs. They were ready to stand up as workers against a powerful company. They were also ready to stand up as free black men against the whole racist society.

12 HARD TIMES

66 *Keep your hands on the plow.* **99**

"Keep Your Hands on the Plow,"
African-American spiritual

It felt to Randolph as if he were running faster and faster but going nowhere. At the beginning of the year, his brother had a raging fever and a gasping cough. Randolph had run from doctor to doctor, trying to find someone who could help. But there was no help. James William Randolph, Jr. died in January 1928 of diphtheria, a throat disease that affects the heart and nerves. He was only 41 years old.

He had been close to graduating from City College and was planning to continue his studies in mathematics and languages at the University of Berlin, in Germany. This was considered one of the best universities in the world.

James had been admired by all those who used to gather at the Randolph house. In fact, James was admired by all who had any contact with him. He was known as one of the most well-read men in New York. Yet he remained modest and shy, completely devoted to his family, and especially to his brother.

In the graveyard, Randolph stared down in terrible grief at the coffin containing his brother's body. Randolph's friends were worried, for he was not in the best of health himself. Later, he wrote a letter to a friend, saying it would be easier to fight a dozen Pullman companies than to overcome his sadness at the death of his beloved brother.

But Randolph hid his feelings behind a calm and kindly mask. He never let on how much he was suffering. One thing drove him on now: to "put the Brotherhood on top."

It had been thought that the new railway labor law would force the company to sit down with the Brotherhood. But it turned out that it did not apply to the railroad porters. There was nothing left for the workers to do but go out on strike.

The threatened strike made news in just about every paper in the country. The members of the Brotherhood had taken a vote on whether to call a strike. The vote was yes: they were ready to walk off the job. This was one of the few times in the history of the country that such a large group of black workers, under black leadership, had made such a threat. There was sympathy for the porters from all classes of people, whites as well as blacks. Thousands volunteered to give food to the porters when they went out on strike. The country was holding its breath.

Still nothing happened. William Green, the white leader of the American Federation of Labor (AFL), a group of almost all the unions in the country, told Randolph that the porters would surely lose if they went out on strike. He said the odds were all against them. Randolph was not sure what to do. So he called off the strike.

The dam broke. The Pullman Company fired everyone it thought had voted for the strike. By 1932, membership in the

Brotherhood had dropped down to only about 770 from a high of about 7,000 in 1928. Offices were closed in Denver, Omaha, Cincinnati, Louisville, and many other cities. It appeared that the union had gone out of existence.

Around the country, the feeling grew that Randolph had deserted or even stabbed the porters in the back. They felt he was wrong to have called off the strike. Almost everybody attacked him. The Negro Labor Congress said that Randolph had really been working for the company, that he had led the porters astray. It said he had never meant there to be a strike in the first place.

The anti-Randolph campaign swept through Chicago. Webster wrote to Randolph, thinking that Randolph was upset and that he should try to make him feel better. But Randolph needed no sympathy. He wrote back to Webster, "Everything moves promisingly forward."

Could Randolph be serious? Had he lost his mind under the strain? Or was he just putting on a brave show?

The *Messenger* now stopped coming out. It was 1928. The porters, feeling betrayed, had turned their backs on it. They stopped reading it. So did other friendly supporters who had helped keep the paper alive, even during its hardest times when the government was attacking it.

In 1926, A. Philip Randolph had applied to get the Brotherhood of Sleeping Car Porters into the American Federation of Labor. He was told by William Green that the porters would have to become part of the union of hotel and restaurant workers. But that union had written into it rules that it would not accept blacks.

But Randolph would not give up. He was aware of the racism in the AFL. In fact, he had written in the *Messenger* years earlier that the American Federation of Labor should be called "The American *Separation* of Labor." He wrote that it was "the most wicked machine for [teaching] race prejudice in the country." But now he felt that if he could join the AFL, he would be able to fight its racism from inside. This was better, he believed, than trying to fight it from the outside.

Finally, Randolph got Green to agree to have the Hotel and Restaurant Workers change their rules to allow the Brotherhood to set up its own organization. This was finally agreed to, and in 1929 the Brotherhood was taken into the AFL. Still, the porters were not treated as equals. But Randolph felt this was the best that could be done for the moment.

On October 29, 1929, the stock market crashed. In just a few days, millions of people had lost all their savings. Many companies went out of business. The Great Depression had begun. Millions upon millions of workers soon lost their jobs. Those who were lucky enough to keep theirs had to work for much less money. Banks failed and people lost their life savings. Millions of farmers lost their land. Millions of city dwellers lost their homes and had to sleep in the streets. The country was in a state of shock.

To most white workers, a depression like this was something new. But for black workers, who had suffered from lack of jobs for years, the Great Depression made things much worse.

White workers who had lost their jobs became so desperate that they were willing to work for any amount of money. So employers fired the black workers and gave white workers their jobs. In the cities, about half of all black workers were out of work. At that time, there was no unemployment insurance from the government to help those out of work. People had to rely on charity. But with so many people needing help, there was just not enough charity to go around.

By 1933 and 1934, the workers who still had jobs began to fight back. They began forming new kinds of unions. These unions were based on the ideas that unions should include everybody, not just skilled workers and not just white men born in the United States. Blacks were now asked to join. These white workers now understood that they could not win without the black workers.

In 1935, the unions within the AFL that shared these beliefs came together and formed the Committee for Industrial Organization (CIO). They were led by the United Mine Workers. They were much more willing to fight for the rights of the workers than the AFL was.

When the CIO was formed, John L. Lewis, its president, offered to help Randolph organize the Brotherhood. In 1935, he invited Randolph to join the new CIO. But Randolph refused. He said he appreciated that the CIO accepted blacks into its unions. But since the AFL still did not, Randolph thought it was important that someone be around to continue to fight for black workers in the AFL. When Lewis offered Randolph lots of money to keep the Brotherhood alive, Randolph thanked him, but he wouldn't take the money. This was one fight, he told Lewis, that blacks had to win all on their own.

So Randolph appealed to the black community for help in saving the Brotherhood. And the community came to the rescue. Money was raised by having picnics and boat rides up the Hudson River. Special concerts were put on, and baseball games. The few people in the black community who had some money set aside lent some of it to Randolph. With Lucille Randolph's help, the wives of the porters formed their own group. They raised more money than anyone else.

Now Randolph felt he could build up the union. He tried to make it look as though the Brotherhood had a lot of money and prestige. He thought this would make the workers feel stronger. When he sent out letters, they were written on the fanciest paper. And at the top of the paper was printed the name of the AFL. Randolph wanted the porters to feel they were not alone anymore, but part of a very powerful group of workers. Still the porters were not happy. They continued to leave the Brotherhood. They didn't believe the Brotherhood had a real chance. Randolph decided to lower the amount of money the porters had to pay to join the union. But that didn't help, either.

The handful of officers that stayed with the Brotherhood

A railroad porter assists a passenger in 1924. By the 1930s, many porters had left the union.

were suffering. Ashley Totten was brought from Kansas City to an easier desk job in New York. He had been beaten to a pulp by thugs. Bennie Smith in Detroit was receiving no money for working for the Brotherhood. Milton Webster lost a job he had in Chicago working for the Republican party. He also lost his job working for the city. His employers said he was spending too much time on activities for the Brotherhood. E. J. Bradley was starving in St. Louis.

Back in New York, the Brotherhood had to close its offices

because it could not pay the mortgage. Randolph watched helplessly as furniture and office records were thrown out by the landlord onto the street.

But the few brave people who, together with Randolph, kept the Brotherhood alive would not give up. Whenever they got discouraged, a picture of Morris "Dad" Moore would flash into their heads. Dad Moore had led the Brotherhood in Oakland, California. He had vowed to stick with the Brotherhood and fight "until Death carry me to my last resting place." Dad Moore passed away at the beginning of 1930.

In one of his last letters, Moore had written that his back was against the wall but he would die before he backed up one inch. He was fighting "not for myself but for 12,000 porters and maids and [their] children." He declared that even though he had been at starvation's door, that he had not changed his mind. "Just as the night follows the [day], we are [going] to win. Tell all the men in your [district] that they should follow Mr. Randolph as they would follow Jesus Christ."

Randolph and those who remained with him could not let the porters down. They could not let Dad Moore down.

The Brotherhood office was moved into an apartment that was Benjamin McLaurin's home. He was a Brotherhood organizer who had come from Chicago. The only way to pay the rent for the apartment was to throw "rent parties." McLaurin cooked great amounts of food and sold it to neighbors and friends who would come to the party. That was their only way of raising money.

There were no secretaries. Everybody had to do his own typing. Sometimes the Brotherhood organizers didn't know where their next meal was coming from. If Randolph had to go on a business trip somewhere, money went to pay for that first. Food would come second. Many days Randolph needed to go somewhere for the Brotherhood, but he couldn't because he didn't have the carfare.

One Christmas, Totten wanted to visit his wife and children

out in Queens, which was only a few miles away from the office. But he didn't even have the few cents it cost to get out there. On Christmas Eve, he and another organizer slept on Randolph's desk. In the night, Totten just broke down and cried.

Randolph had so many patches on his pants that there wasn't room for one more. He had no soles on his shoes. One day, seeing the terrible condition of his one remaining shirt, two friends of the Brotherhood went out and bought Randolph a couple of new ones. They said, "We ain't going to let him speak with that shirt on."

One time, Mayor Fiorello La Guardia of New York offered Randolph a job.

"Phil," he said, "you have holes in your shoes. It will take a lifetime to organize the porters. Take a job with the city. You need to eat and pay your rent. You can carry out your organizing activities while you work for the city."

But Randolph turned the job down. He said he already had a job.

That was just like Randolph. To others, he seemed quite crazy. Everybody thought the Brotherhood was dead. Everybody but Randolph. He just kept on doing his job. Nothing could break him. No one could buy him. He continued to travel around the country with whatever money the porters could scrape together.

He talked about the rights of porters to have decent pay, health care, and shorter working hours. But he spoke up, too, for all workers, for an end to segregation, for the rights of mothers to have help in child care. He spoke on behalf of all who were not treated fairly.

Randolph went on talking about the union. For him, unions were the key that would allow workers to control their own lives. And Randolph never lost hope that one day the porters would have their own strong union.

FIGHTING BACK

> **❝ Before I'd be a slave, I'll be buried in my grave. ❞**

"No More Mourning,"
African-American
spiritual

Republican President Herbert Hoover kept telling the people that good times were right around the corner. But the depression just kept dragging on and getting even worse. The year 1930 passed. Then 1931. The election for the next president of the United States was held at the end of 1932, and Democrat Franklin Delano Roosevelt won in a landslide.

When Roosevelt took office in 1933, business was in ruins. The factory and shop owners were having a hard time. But for the working people, it was sheer disaster. Early in the depression, the workers had been confused. They hadn't known what to do. They had thought maybe things would get back to normal in a little while. Then, when things got no better, they began to get angry. They saw that the government didn't seem to care about them. They saw rich people having great parties and "living it up" while the working people were hungry.

The workers started marching in the streets. They had demonstrations. Those who had no jobs formed groups called unemployed councils. They demanded help from the government for themselves and their families. Often they marched into government offices, sat down, and would not leave until they were given money or food or other help. When landlords tried to force people out of their homes, the neighbors picked up the furniture that the landlord had thrown out into the streets and carried it right back into the houses. Those who were told they couldn't live there anymore just stayed on anyhow.

The people told the politicians that they wanted action. The government, they said, should protect the people from hunger and from the cold. They told the politicians that the government should provide jobs for those who didn't have them.

Roosevelt heard the voice of the American people. He had said that when he became president he would bring in a New Deal. His new administration immediately began to take action. Its goal was to try to end the Great Depression and get business going again. It was pledged to keep the people from starving.

Among the first laws that the government passed was the National Industrial Recovery Act. Another law, which Randolph felt was very important to the Pullman porters, was the Emergency Railroad Transportation Act. What these two laws said, among other things, was that companies could no longer force people who worked for them to join the company unions.

In the past, companies had set up special groups that pretended to be unions but really were not. These unions were

totally under the control of the companies. Naturally, they could not be used by the workers to fight the companies. If workers in a company tried to form a real union, they were told that the company already had a union. The workers were then forced to join the company union.

But now, thanks to the new laws, companies couldn't do that anymore. The workers could organize their own unions. They could now send their own representatives to the meetings with the owners to demand what they really needed.

When the new laws were passed, there was great excitement in the country, especially among the working people. The *New York Times*, the leading newspaper in the country, said that labor had suddenly jumped into power. William Green called the new laws labor's Bill of Rights. John L. Lewis said the new labor laws freed labor, just as President Abraham Lincoln's order had freed the slaves.

New unions were being formed all over the United States. Before Roosevelt's election, the workers had felt that the government would always be against them. But now the union leaders told workers that Roosevelt wanted them to organize.

The Pullman porters took courage and they began coming back to the Brotherhood. Randolph had great hopes now. He wrote to the Pullman Company, asking the company to sit down and talk with him and other Brotherhood leaders about making an agreement.

Randolph waited. But no answer came.

Again, it turned out that the Pullman Company could wiggle out of dealing with the Brotherhood. The new law somehow still did not cover the porters.

Randolph swung into action. He went all out to get Congress to fix the law so that it would protect the Pullman porters, too. In 1934, a new version of the Railway Labor Act was passed. But the Pullman Company wasn't sleeping either. It wanted to avoid obeying the law. Seeing that Randolph was winning lots of friends in Congress, the company fired many porters and hired new ones. But in order to get their jobs, the new workers had to join the Pullman Porters Protection Association. This group had been formed secretly by the company with a few frightened porters who would do anything their bosses told them to do. Now, the company, pointing to the small group of porters it controlled, said that this was the real union. The company said that it would not, therefore, deal with the Brotherhood.

Randolph demanded that the government put an end to this trick. The government then decided to hold elections to find out whom the porters really wanted. In June 1935, votes were taken in over 60 towns and cities around the country. This was the moment of truth! The results were announced: only 1,422 people had voted for the Protection Association; 8,316 had voted for Randolph's Brotherhood. Webster, Totten, and the other Brotherhood officers were overjoyed. But this was more than just a union victory. As Randolph said in his telegram to Walter White, the head of the NAACP, "This is the first victory of Negro workers over a great...corporation."

Another powerful organization of black people, the Urban League, said when it heard the news of the Brotherhood victory: "No labor leadership in America has faced greater odds. None has won a greater victory."

On July 29, 1935, A. Philip Randolph, his heart racing, marched into the head office of the Pullman Company in Chicago to meet with A. J. Curry, Pullman's president. By Randolph's side were Webster, Bennie Smith, E. J. Bradley, C. L. Dellums, and two working porters—all men who had fought side by side with Randolph for so long. After 10 years of what Randolph had been told over and over again was a hopeless and foolish struggle, the high and mighty Pullman Company had to face the Brotherhood. A. J. Curry had to sit down at the same table with a "bunch of black porters."

Randolph and his group were nervous the first few moments they sat across the table from Curry, the lawyers, and others who had important jobs in the company. But it wasn't long before they forgot about how nervous they were and just fought it out at the table with the Pullman people.

At first the Pullman side tried to fool the Brotherhood with all kinds of tricks. But in 1937, the United States Supreme Court ruled that the 1934 version of the Railway Labor Act had to be obeyed. After that, at last, on August 25, 1937, Curry said, "Gentlemen, the Pullman Company is ready to sign."

And sign they did. It was the first agreement ever signed between a union of black workers and a large American company. Under the agreement, the workers got a very large wage increase. Their working hours were cut from 400 a month to 240. And the company gave in on other things that had caused so many problems for the porters for so long.

All across America, A. Philip Randolph made the news. He became a celebrity, the most popular black political figure in the

United States. Expecting the Brotherhood to win, William Green had a year earlier allowed the Brotherhood to be part of the AFL as an equal member, with all the rights that the other unions had. Mayor LaGuardia of New York called Randolph "one of the most progressive labor leaders in America."

Naturally, Randolph was happy at his success. For a moment he felt as though a great weight had been lifted from his shoulders. But only for a moment. For he knew how much remained to be done to better the lot of his people. He knew he had only scratched the surface, even in the labor movement. He knew that while the porters were now organized, the greatest number of black workers were still outside the unions. Furthermore, Jim Crow laws still existed in the South. And lynchings were still going on. And...and...and... There was no end to the list of evils that had to be faced.

There were many other black leaders who felt just as Randolph did. These were new leaders coming up who thought the old leaders were not doing enough to help black people. They felt the older leaders were too slow-moving, not willing to take chances. What was needed was a new fighting organization, one that would bring people out into the streets to march and demonstrate. That organization, the National Negro Congress, held its first meeting in Chicago in February 1936. The congress had been formed by a number of people who were looked up to in the black community, people like Ralph Bunche and Alain Locke, who were professors at Howard University. Bunche would later have the second highest job in the United Nations. Locke was an outstanding person in the field of black literature and philosophy. Also issuing the call was John P. Davis, a very fine newspaper writer.

Randolph was asked to become president of the National Negro Congress. He was nominated by Adam Clayton Powell, Jr., a man who later became the most powerful black politician in the United States.

At the Chicago meeting were people from over 500 political,

religious, labor, and other organizations. More than 5,000 visitors were on hand, including a large number of white people. Randolph accepted the presidency with pleasure. Nothing pleased him more. The National Negro Congress was going to organize black workers into unions. The congress had many powerful friends. Randolph was now in charge of a group that seemed much stronger than the Brotherhood.

Of course, Randolph still had many duties as the Brotherhood's leader. He had to work on finishing up the agreement with the Pullman Company. He had to take charge of Brother-

Rep. Adam Clayton Powell insisted that a desegregation clause be attached to any federal funds.

hood meetings. He had to make many speeches around the country, for everyone wanted to hear him. He needed to spend time with his wife, whom he depended on for love and for the wonderful kindness and strength she always gave him. Through all their years together, their love for each other burned as brightly as ever.

Being as busy as he was, and not in the best of health, Randolph was not always as close to what was going on in the National Negro Congress as he would have liked. The day-to-day running of the organization he left to others. He did not pay attention at first when people began to complain to him that the congress had been taken over by Communists. For many of the enemies of the black people labeled as "Communist" anyone or anything that helped black people. Besides, he had worked with Communists in the past, and he felt that the National Negro Congress should include different political groups.

In 1939, war broke out in Europe once again. One country after another was brought into the conflict, until it became a world war—World War II. Dangerous men had come to power in a number of countries in Europe—in Germany, Italy, and Spain. German armies, led by the Nazi dictator Adolf Hitler, overran a number of countries, and were getting ready to conquer others.

Randolph had been against the United States taking part in World War I back in 1917. But he felt that this time the situation was different. This war had to do with fighting fascism. Fascism stood for the idea that there were master races and slave races. One fascist belief was that a few nations should rule the world. Supporters of fascism believed that people should have no rights, that they should blindly follow their leaders. Randolph saw fascism as the greatest evil to all the peoples of the world, but especially to the peoples of the world who were not white. He agreed with President Franklin D. Roosevelt that the United States should build up its defenses. There seemed very little chance that the United States could keep out of the war.

Randolph said all this when he spoke at the 1940 meeting of the National Negro Congress. But in the middle of his speech, people in the audience started to boo him. He was shocked. When he finished his speech, the National Negro Congress members went on to vote against preparing for war. They believed the war was unjust and that the United States should stay out of it. This was what the Communist party believed, but it was not what many black organizations believed. Randolph decided that the Communists had indeed taken over the congress.

In an angry speech in which he said he was leaving the congress, he attacked the Communists for having taken over. He said the black people needed to control their own organizations. As he spoke, three-quarters of the people in the hall walked out. Not long after that, the National Negro Congress went out of existence.

The congress fell apart, but A. Philip Randolph was moving ahead. As a matter of fact, he began to plan something that would really shake the country up.

14 A. PHILIP RANDOLPH— HERO

❝ *I wouldn't take nothing for my journey now.* **❞**

Old church saying

All through the 1930s, in spite of all the things the government tried to do to get things moving again, the Great Depression had still hung on. Millions of workers still had not found jobs. There were more than twice as many blacks out of work as whites. And when blacks tried to get help from the government, they were not treated fairly.

In 1940 and 1941, the situation got better. Factories opened up to start making the planes and ships, the guns, electrical equipment, and other goods needed for defense. Factories also made things for our European friends who needed them for the war. So millions of workers found jobs again. But these new war jobs were not open to blacks. Instead of doing better, because the president was supposed to be a friend of theirs, black people were going backward, and fast! Blacks asked themselves, were they again going to be called upon to give up their lives for their country, to shoot guns in foreign lands—guns that they were not even allowed to make at home? How many more years would black people have to wait for justice?

The New York hall was packed and still as A. Philip Randolph, standing straight, as always, and calm, threw out his challenge to the president, to the Congress, and to the people of the United States. His message that night in September 1940 was printed in thousands of leaflets that had been spread across the nation. It was a call to black people, a loud, ringing call.

"We call upon you," Randolph said to the people, "to fight for jobs in national defense. We call upon you to fight for the right of African Americans to fight alongside whites in the armed forces of the nation. We call upon you to march to put an end to all Jim Crow laws, all separation of blacks from whites, in all government departments and in defense jobs."

The audience in the hall that night was made up of the men and women from the Brotherhood of Sleeping Car Porters. They had come from all over the United States to hear this important message from Randolph. Among them, one white woman stood out. It was clear that she was listening with great attention. She had come to attend this special 15th anniversary meeting of the Brotherhood. Her name was Eleanor Roosevelt, and she was the First Lady, the wife of the president.

Mrs. Roosevelt had been asked to speak the following night at a special Brotherhood dinner. But on this day, she was only observing.

The porters voted unanimously to back this effort. When the results of the vote were read out loud, everybody began clapping loudly and cheering. Mrs. Roosevelt was clapping, too, and her warm smile took in the whole room. When she spoke the next evening, she promised to help do anything "to make this a better country, not for you alone but for all of us."

Mrs. Roosevelt didn't waste any time. She must have spoken to the president as soon as she got back to Washington. Two days later, she telephoned the president's secretary, Steve Early, and told him that the president wanted a meeting right away. He wanted to meet with under secretary of war Patterson and secretary of the navy Knox. Mrs. Roosevelt told Steve Early that the president was going to be talking about the rights of blacks to join the army. Also to be invited to the meeting was Walter White of the NAACP, T. Arnold Hill of the National Urban League, and A. Philip Randolph.

Randolph, White, and Hill came to that meeting at the White House. They brought with them a written statement calling for black people to be brought into everything having to do with defending the country, whether it be the army or navy or the factories making goods for the war.

Roosevelt nodded for Randolph to speak. Here he was, face to face with the president of the United States. What a long road he had traveled. Randolph was very direct. He did not beat around the bush.

Randolph wanted the law of the land to make sure that his people would be rid of racism. Black people had been through enough suffering and the president had it in his power to do something about it. For example, Randolph said, the president could issue a special order to make it illegal for blacks to be kept separate in the army and navy. He could also issue an order that would make it illegal for factory owners to refuse to hire blacks when they got money from the government to make war goods.

Randolph was sure that there were many whites of good will in the country who needed only a little support from the president to do the right things. Randolph knew that there were many whites on his side, people like Mrs. Roosevelt.

The president was polite, smiled, and was very charming. When the meeting was over, the black leaders felt encouraged, although the president had not really made any promises.

Two weeks later, the president's secretary, Steve Early, called the newspapers in to talk to them. "You will remember," he said,

A. Philip Randolph with Eleanor Roosevelt (center).

"that . . . . the President held a conference with Walter White and I think two other Negro leaders . . . . As a result of this, the War Department had drafted [prepared] a statement of policy with regard to Negroes in national defense." Then Early handed out the paper with the statement on it.

Randolph sat in his office and read that statement over and over again. It said that the War Department was not going to mix black and white soldiers and sailors in the same units. So it was still the same old segregation. The way Early had given out the statement, and the way the newspapers were reporting the story, it seemed as if Walter White and the "two other Negro leaders" had agreed to all this. It was a lie, but would black people believe the lie?

Not long after this, a black policeman trying to protect the president, who was visiting New York City, was kicked by a white man breaking through the police lines. That white man turned out later to be none other than Steve Early. Black people now demanded that the president get rid of Early. But he refused.

Meanwhile, White, Randolph, and Hill were trying to straighten out the confusion caused by Early's lie. They began doing a lot of letter writing, making speeches, and holding meetings with newspapers to clear their names and to make sure everyone understood that they did *not* support segregation in the armed forces.

Finally, the three leaders received a letter from Roosevelt apologizing for what he called a misunderstanding. "The plan.... on which we are all agreed," he wrote, "is that Negroes will be put into all branches of the service, combatant [fighting] as well as supply." Roosevelt also spoke about allowing blacks to train in the air force and said that they would have a chance to become officers.

But the president had not touched on the main point. The real question was, Were blacks going to be segregated or not? And were they going to be hired to make war goods?

It was while traveling south with Milton Webster to visit some of the Brotherhood groups that the thoughts which he had been turning over and over in his mind finally became very clear to Randolph.

"You know, Web," he said, "calling on the President and holding those conferences are not going to get us any-where.... We are going to have to do something about it."

Webster thought to himself, "Here it comes again. Brother Randolph [is] always figuring out something for us to do, sticking his nose in everything to see where he can stir something up." But Webster knew he would be going right along with Randolph. He said nothing.

Randolph pressed on: "I think we ought to get 10,000 Negroes to march on Washington in protest, march down Pennsylvania Avenue. What do you think of that?"

Webster had to catch his breath. "Where are you going to get 10,000 Negroes?"

"I think we can get them" is all that Randolph said. And he sank back in silence for the rest of the trip.

In Savannah, Georgia, Randolph called a public meeting and announced his plan for a march on Washington. People couldn't make up their minds whether to be scared or excited, so they were both.

From Savannah, Randolph and Webster went on to Jacksonville, Tampa, and Miami, preaching all the way about the march. Black newspapers picked up the story, and even though most white newspapers didn't print a word about it, by the time Randolph got back to New York the idea had really caught fire.

On January 15, 1941, Randolph told all the newspapers about the planned march. Immediately, the Brotherhood offices were swamped with mail. People wanted to know how they could help. They wanted to know how they could get things together in their part of the country.

Randolph called for help from the NAACP and the Urban League. If anyone else had suggested the idea to them, those two organizations would probably have laughed it off. But since it was A. Philip Randolph's idea, it was to be taken seriously. Both groups agreed to join forces with Randolph.

A March on Washington Committee was formed. Randolph was the director. People who wanted to work for the committee came from all over, but it was the Brotherhood members who played the most important role. They raised money and helped with every problem that came up. The date of the march was set for July 1, 1941. By the end of May, Randolph was not only sure of getting 10,000 blacks to march, but he thought there would be over 100,000. "Let the Negro masses speak," said Randolph, and his cry was heard around the country.

The White House became worried. Would Randolph dare? Such a march would be terribly embarrassing to the president. The country was about to get into the war in Europe, and he didn't want anything to happen that would divide the people. Of course, the split was already there. It was not black people who were causing it.

Randolph continued to prepare for the march. It seemed clear that it was going to be very big. Somebody would have to talk Randolph out of it, the president thought. So Roosevelt sent two people to Randolph that he knew Randolph respected: Mayor Fiorello La Guardia and Eleanor Roosevelt. Both LaGuardia and Mrs. Roosevelt did their best. They warned of possible violence. They said the march would make the country angry, would do more harm than good.

But it was no use. Randolph's mind was made up, and nothing was going to stand in the way of the demonstration.

In the end, it was not Randolph who backed down. It was the president of the United States. Six days before the march was to take place, President Roosevelt issued Executive Order 8802. This order made it a crime for companies that were getting money from government contracts to refuse to hire blacks. Also, a Fair Employment Practices Committee was set up to see to it that the president's order was carried out.

When Randolph learned of the order, he called off the march. But he kept the March on Washington Committee going, just in case.

Praise came pouring in from all sides. The New York *Amsterdam News* said Randolph ranked "along with the great Frederick Douglass.... We regard A. Philip Randolph as the man of the hour." W. E. B. Du Bois, who had always been Randolph's hero, called Randolph's achievement "astonishing." Others called him an American Gandhi, a comparison to the great nonviolent leader of the people of India.

Blacks across the country were thrilled. For one of the few times in their memory, they felt a sense of power and pride.

As things turned out, it was one thing to have an order on paper and quite another to actually get the jobs. The jobs came very slowly. Many employers refused to obey the order. The government did not seem in a big hurry to see to it that they did obey it.

Suddenly, on December 7, 1941, the news came over the radio that the Japanese had attacked the American naval base at Pearl Harbor in Hawaii and had sunk many U.S. warships.

And so war came. Millions of young men were drafted into the armed forces. As they left and as the demands for the war goods on the factories kept growing, there was a great shortage of labor. There just weren't enough workers to make what was needed. It was then that large numbers of black workers finally got their chance to get jobs.

Although the march on Washington had been called off, Randolph had told his followers that the movement would continue. One June 16, 1942, more than 20,000 people filled Madison Square Garden in New York City to greet A. Philip Randolph.

As he moved up the aisle, surrounded by 100 uniformed porters in front and 50 Pullman maids behind, the entire crowd stood up. The clapping was so loud that it was almost impossible to hear the Brotherhood marching band play the union's battle song, "Hold the Fort for We Are Coming." Randolph said later that it was "the biggest demonstration of Negroes in the history of the world."

Randolph did not speak—there wasn't enough time for his speech—Adam Clayton Powell, Jr., took the microphone and announced that he was running for Congress. Powell did run, and he won. He became the first black man to represent Harlem in Congress. There was little doubt that he owed a great debt to Randolph for his success.

STANDING UP TO ANOTHER PRESIDENT

> ❝ *Talk about just as much as you please. Nothing's going to bring me to my knees.* ❞
>
> "Hold the Wind, Don't Let It Blow,"
> African-American spiritual

Everything in the country was now set up for the war effort. There were many changes in the way the country did things. But certain things did not change. There was still racial discrimination and segregation, including in the armed forces.

The war was a war for democracy. It was a war against fascism, against the claim of the German Nazis to be a superior race. The Nazis had already killed millions of people because they believed them to be racially "inferior," including millions of Jews and other Europeans.

There was no superior race, said the U.S. government. But at the same time, black people in the United States continued to be treated like an inferior race.

Black people had done much for the American victory. They had shed their blood on foreign soil. They were very brave on the battlefield. They worked hard at home to help win the war. Now they looked forward to a new day. They felt the United States could not possibly go back to the old ways. They vowed that black people would never bow their heads low again. They expected that they would now receive their full rights as American citizens.

It turned out that they were half-right and half-wrong. They were wrong because the country did try to settle back into the old ways of doing things. Whites tried to put blacks back into their usual place, and there was a lot of violence, especially in the South. They were as much as saying, "Hey, you may have been a big shot when you carried a rifle in Europe and Asia, but you're nothing to us here, and you'd better get used to it."

But the black people who said a new day was coming were also right. For something important had happened to the spirit of black people. There was a new pride among blacks. For they had made up their minds that things were *not* going to go back to the old ways. This spirit would build quietly until about 10 years after the war it exploded in the giant civil rights movement.

In the late 1940s, people wanted to go back to a peaceful life after the bloody world war. But almost immediately, the war drums began beating again. Now Americans were told that communism and the Soviet Union were their enemies. It was thought that the United States was in great danger again.

When Roosevelt died in 1945, Vice-President Harry Truman became president. He called for a draft again, to require young men to enter military service. Although Randolph had been very unhappy about segregation in the armed forces during

World War II, he had not called for marches because he did not want anything to harm the life-and-death struggle with the Nazis.

But now Truman was calling for a draft in a time of peace. The army and navy were still segregated. To fight this, Randolph formed in 1947 the Committee Against Jim Crow in Military Service and Training. A year later, the name was changed to the League for Nonviolent Civil Disobedience Against Military Segregation. By disobeying the country's law, the organizers wanted to defeat the draft bill in Congress because it did not ban segregation in the armed forces. Randolph invited Bayard Rustin to help organize the new committee.

Rustin had had a great deal of experience working for one of the most important peace groups in the country called the Fellowship of Reconciliation. He had also helped organize CORE, the Congress of Racial Equality, which had been formed with the help of the fellowship. Rustin had helped Randolph back in the days of the planned 1941 March on Washington. During the war, he had refused to be drafted because of his opposition to the war. As a result he was forced to spend nearly three years in a federal prison. Rustin would later become the chief organizer of the great March on Washington in 1963.

Relations with the Soviet Union kept getting worse. President Truman knew that Randolph was a very serious man, one who was not in the habit of bluffing. If Randolph succeeded in defeating the draft bill, it would damage the position of the United States in the world.

So, in March 1948, after Randolph had made it quite clear that the campaign not to obey the government would begin, Truman invited a group of black leaders to the White House. Randolph was among them.

The meeting got off to a friendly start. But when it was his turn to speak, Randolph looked President Truman straight in the eye and told him, "Mr. President, after making several trips around the country, I can tell you that the mood among Negroes of this country is that they will never bear arms again until all forms of bias and discrimination are abolished."

Harry Truman was also known as a straight talker. He told Randolph, "I wish you hadn't made that statement. I don't like it at all."

Attorney Charles Houston, who was working with the NAACP, then spoke up: "But Mr. President, don't you want to know what is happening in the country?"

Truman had to admit he needed to know the truth.

"Well...," Randolph went on, "I'm giving you the facts. Mr. President, as you know, we are calling upon you to issue an executive order abolishing [ending] segregation in the armed forces."

Truman tried to be polite. But everyone could see he was burning inside. He suddenly thanked them all for coming and said he didn't think there was much more they could talk about together. The group was then led out of Truman's office.

Randolph was then called upon to speak before the committee in the U.S. Senate that had to draw up a new law on the draft. Randolph did not bite his tongue. "This time," he told the committee, "Negroes will not take a Jim Crow draft lying down."

He warned the senators that people around the world would turn against the United States if they saw thousands upon thousands of black people choose to go to prison rather than go into "military slavery," as second-class citizens. "I personally will advise Negroes to refuse to fight as slaves for a democracy they cannot possess and enjoy."

The storm clouds were gathering. The government knew Randolph wasn't only speaking for himself. Word had come from around the country that blacks who fought for their country in the last war were really angry. A number of white youths were ready to fight the draft, too.

One of the senators tried to get Randolph to confess to being a traitor, an enemy of the United States. Of course, Randolph knew he was no traitor. There was no way in the world anyone could make black people believe that Randolph was a traitor. Nor did most of the country believe it.

When Randolph finished speaking to the senators, he stopped by at the March on Washington headquarters. He told his people there, "I am prepared to oppose a Jim Crow army until I rot in jail."

Randolph was a man of his word. He started to speak at a number of meetings on the corner of 125th Street and Seventh Avenue, the most famous block in Harlem. Crowds always came there to hear truths they could never find in the white-owned newspapers or on the white-owned radio. Randolph told the young men who faced the draft to refuse to go into the army. By choosing a path of civil disobedience, Randolph knew he was going against the law, but he felt that he had to obey a higher law, a moral law.

Not everyone in the black community agreed with Randolph. But Congressman Adam Clayton Powell, Jr., came out strongly for him. Congressman Powell wrote a letter to the senators who had been questioning Randolph. He told them that Randolph was really saying the things that were on the minds of 15 million African Americans. And he added, "We are not going to be frightened by the cry of 'Treason.' If the finger of treason can be pointed at anyone, it must be pointed at those of you who are traitors to our Constitution and to our Bill of Rights. There aren't enough jails in America to hold the Colored people who will refuse to bear arms in a Jim Crow army."

But the most powerful backing for Randolph came not from any black leader but from the young black men themselves who actually faced the draft. When asked to give their opinion, three out of four young men in Harlem said that they would disobey the government and not go into the army, if called.

In July 1948, the Democratic National Convention was meeting in Philadelphia. There was a big battle going on inside

In the 1940s, A. Philip Randolph successfully fought against a segregated, or "Jim Crow," army.

between the Democrats from the South who felt that their party was "giving too much" to black people, and the liberals who felt that the party was going too slowly on civil rights.

Everyone in the hall was aware that outside, marching back and forth with large signs, shouting their demands, were A. Philip Randolph and his followers. One of their signs read "Prison Is Better Than Army Jim Crow Service!"

The politicians were worried. They didn't know what to do. There just didn't seem to be any good answers.

Thanks to Randolph's work, thanks to the liberals who backed civil rights, and thanks to the millions around the world who stood with African Americans, President Truman gave in. On July 26, 1948, he signed Executive Order 9981. Under this order, blacks were to be treated exactly the same as whites in the army and navy.

A. Philip Randolph by now knew very well how presidents could use words to mean one thing when they really meant another. Randolph was going to make sure this time that there was no way the government would be able to slip through on its promises as it had done before. So he got in touch with the White House and asked whether the executive order meant to get rid of discrimination and segregation.

Truman sent word that the order did indeed make segregation illegal.

Satisfied, Randolph told the young men it was now all right to obey the government and to go into the army.

Was it tongue in cheek and with a twinkle in his eyes that Randolph sent a telegram praising the president for his "high order of statesmanship and courage"?

16 VICTORIES

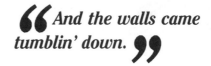

> **And the walls came tumblin' down.**
>
> "Joshua and the Battle of Jericho,"
> African-American spiritual

Asa and Lucille rejoiced together over the victories won by getting two U.S. presidents to change their policies. They were warmed by praise pouring in from all over the country and even around the world. Still, so much remained to be done. The condition of black people remained bad. Lucille was in such pain from arthritis that she had to be kept in a wheelchair. But this did not stop her from urging Asa on. A. Philip Randolph was more than ever ready to carry on the struggle.

The NAACP and other groups had gone to the courts over and over again to see if they could get some justice there. Many times they asked the courts to put an end to segregation in the South. But the courts had turned them down so many times. Now, however, there was a new spirit in the air since the end of World War II, and it was felt that maybe the courts would see things in a new way. Some small victories had been won. But then, in 1954, the Supreme Court of the United States made a ruling in a case called *Brown* v. *Board of Education of Topeka* (Kansas) that absolutely shook the southern system of schooling.

What the Court said was that there was no such thing as "separate but equal." Any kind of segregation was unequal and inferior, so segregated education was inferior education. And the Supreme Court said that this was against the U.S. Constitution.

A storm broke out in the South. In a few towns and cities, the schools were integrated very quickly, with little trouble. But in many other places in the South, the governors and local officials swore that they would never allow integration. Some communities closed down the public schools and then reopened them as "private" schools so that they would not have to obey the law concerning public schools.

It looked as if the country might be moving toward a new civil war. The governors of the southern states were using their state troopers and National Guardsmen to keep black children out of the all-white schools. Southern mayors fought integration by using their local police. Black people and their white friends demanded that the president send in federal marshals and troops to enforce the new law of the land.

While all this was going on, the body of a small 14-year-old black boy was found floating in the waters along a Mississippi town. When they pulled him out, they saw that one of his eyes had been gouged out. He had been shot in the head and horribly tortured. This boy, Emmett Till, had come to Mississippi in 1955 from Chicago to visit his relatives. He was lynched because he had dared say "Bye, Baby," to a white woman in a store.

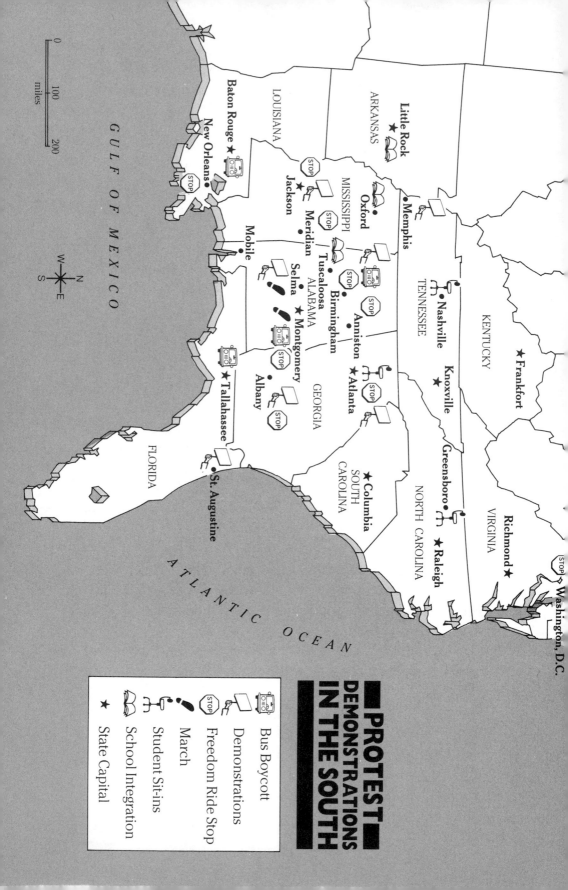

PROTEST DEMONSTRATIONS IN THE SOUTH

Legend:

- 🚌 Bus Boycott
- Demonstrations
- 🛑 Freedom Ride Stop
- March
- Student Sit-ins
- ★ School Integration
- ★ State Capital

Scale: 0 — 100 — 200 miles

Compass: N, S, E, W

Water bodies: GULF OF MEXICO, ATLANTIC OCEAN

States and Cities:

- ARKANSAS — Little Rock
- LOUISIANA — Baton Rouge ★, New Orleans
- MISSISSIPPI — Oxford, Jackson ★, Meridian
- TENNESSEE — Memphis, Nashville, Knoxville
- KENTUCKY — Frankfort ★
- ALABAMA — Tuscaloosa, Birmingham, Selma, Montgomery ★, Anniston, Mobile
- GEORGIA — Atlanta ★, Albany
- FLORIDA — Tallahassee ★, St. Augustine
- SOUTH CAROLINA — Columbia ★
- NORTH CAROLINA — Greensboro, Raleigh ★
- VIRGINIA — Richmond ★
- Washington, D.C.

A. Philip Randolph was involved in all the struggles of African Americans. So was Lucille. She had been very active in a number of organizations and had used her energy to raise money to help those struggles and to try to get people to join the freedom movement. Now, she could do little more than talk from her bedside. Lucille's health was fading. She was in constant pain. Randolph stayed at home with her as much as possible to relieve her of as many tasks as he could. They still called each other "Buddy." He prepared their meals and treated her with great tenderness.

One day in 1955, a black woman named Rosa Parks refused to give up her seat on the bus to a white person in Montgomery, Alabama, as the law demanded. Rosa Parks was put in jail. When a local black women's group heard about this, its members decided the time had come to take up the fight against this kind of treatment of black people. With the help of E. D. Nixon, a past president of the local NAACP, they asked the local black ministers to help. This group chose the Reverend Martin Luther King, Jr., to lead them.

Thus began what is considered the first great event of the modern civil rights movement. The black people of Montgomery refused to ride the city buses for over a year. Many people walked back and forth to work and all around the city. It reminded Randolph of the decision his father had made about half a century before not to ride the carriages in Jacksonville.

Randolph was proud of all the black people in Montgomery, and he was especially proud that it was his friend E. D. Nixon, also the Montgomery president of the Brotherhood of Sleeping Car Porters, who had played an important part in the boycott.

Whenever there was a struggle for freedom anywhere in the country, somebody would be sure to call A. Philip Randolph for advice and help. He was always in the thick of things, even if he could not always be right there personally, for he himself was not in the best of health, and he had to take care of Lucille, too. Randolph was now being called the "Father of the Civil Rights Movement" and it seemed just the right title for him.

In 1957, Randolph went with Dr. King to demonstrate in Washington. In 1957 and 1958, Randolph organized two youth marches on Washington, where thousands of young people protested that the Supreme Court ruling against segregated schooling was not being carried out.

In 1959, Randolph attended the national meeting of the AFL-CIO. The AFL and the CIO had been fighting each other for years. But finally, the two groups had joined together and Randolph became one of its vice-presidents in 1957.

Randolph fought within the AFL for years against its racism. Year after year, he would get up on the AFL convention floor and make his lonely call for justice for black workers. Year after year, the union leaders would turn him down.

Now that the AFL and CIO were joined, Randolph thought he had a better chance. The civil rights movement was growing stronger every day, and the union leaders had to move with the times.

One of the unions within the old federation had been thrown out a few years earlier for corruption. That was the International Longshoremen's Association. Now they wanted to be allowed back into the AFL-CIO. Randolph knew that not only had it been a corrupt union whose leaders were thought to have stolen a lot of money from the members, but it was one of the most racist unions. Randolph saw his chance. He would agree to let the Longshoremen come back in, but they had to promise to end their racist treatment of black and Puerto Rican workers.

George Meany, the new head of the AFL-CIO, became very angry at Randolph. Turning to Randolph, he exploded: "Who appointed you the guardian of the Negro members in America?"

Some people at the meeting tried to come to Randolph's defense. But the AFL-CIO leadership voted to condemn Randolph, one of the saddest moments in the history of trade unions.

Randolph did not take this lying down. It was not just Randolph who had been insulted. It was all the black people. Right

A. Philip Randolph meets here with George Meany (center) president of the AFL–CIO.

after that, Randolph formed a new organization to fight racism in the unions. It was called the Negro American Labor Council. The council tried to help black workers get jobs and managed to do so in a number of cases. Randolph gave strength to the civil rights movement. In turn, the civil rights movement gave him strength. Two years later, George Meany was forced to apologize to Randolph for his behavior. At the next national meeting of the AFL-CIO in 1959, it was voted that they would work harder to make sure all Americans in every field of life were treated equally. This meant in the labor unions, too.

Lucille's health got worse every day. Randolph was extremely worried. She died in March 1963. In Randolph's public world, the cause of freedom for black people was everything. In his personal world, Lucille was everything. He had never stopped loving her. The great March on Washington was to take place in just a few months. Randolph was an important part of that march. Would he be able to carry on his work without her?

Bayard Rustin, one of the men closest to Randolph, helped him get back on his feet. They had worked closely together for the past 15 years. Rustin looked up to A. Philip Randolph, and through the years he could never address him except respectfully as "Mr. Randolph." Bayard was like a son to Randolph. Now 52 himself, Rustin could still do things it would be hard for several men to do. Very bright and talented, Rustin was happy to work quietly in Randolph's shadow. He had paid a heavy price for his principles. Twenty years earlier he had been savagely beaten by police in Tennessee when he had refused to ride in the back of a bus. During World War II, he had spent three years in prison because he did not believe in violence and would not serve in the army. In 1947, he had spent almost a month in a North Carolina chain gang after being arrested as one of the first Freedom Riders.

Rustin was a great organizer. He had helped to organize big events not only in the United States but in India and Africa, as well.

It was in a conversation between Randolph and Rustin that the idea of a great March on Washington in 1963 first came up. Randolph approved of the great demonstrations for civil rights that Dr. King was leading in the South. But both he and Rustin felt that the economic struggle was important, too—the struggle for jobs, for a higher minimum wage, and for a guaranteed income for everyone in the country. It was decided that the march should be for both jobs and freedom. Randolph then got in touch with the Reverend Martin Luther King, Jr., and Roy Wilkins of the NAACP.

The plan was to bring 100,000 people to Washington on August 28, 1963. The whole thing was being run by Rustin from a rundown little office in Harlem. There wasn't much money to advertise and tell about the march. There were very few people working in the office. It seemed impossible that such a huge demonstration would take place.

Once again, a president of the United States wanted the march called off. This time it was John F. Kennedy. Once again,

The March on Washington

During the 1940s, A. Philip Randolph planned two marches on Washington, D.C. He wanted to protest unfair hiring practices in the government work place and segregation in the military. Both times, his demands were met, and so the marches were called off.

Then in 1963, Randolph organized another march on the Capital. This time it was to put pressure on Congress to pass a new civil rights bill. Over 250,000 people joined in the demonstration.

In 1925, Randolph had formed the Brotherhood of Sleeping Car Porters. The Brotherhood was the first labor union for African Americans in this country. He worked hard to get the white labor unions to accept the Brotherhood into their organizations. For the 1963 march, Randolph was able to bring together civil rights and labor leaders, both black and white, to fight against racism.

Randolph marches with Roy Wilkins of NAACP and Walter Reuther, president of United Auto Workers.

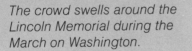

The crowd swells around the
Lincoln Memorial during the
March on Washington.

Randolph at the Lincoln
Memorial with other civil rights
leaders during the March on
Washington.

President Kennedy helped Randolph and other labor
leaders to improve working conditions.

a meeting was held between a president and black leaders in the
White House.

The group included Dr. Martin Luther King, Jr., John Lewis
of the Student Nonviolent Coordinating Committee (SNCC),
James Farmer of CORE, Roy Wilkins of the NAACP, and, of
course, A. Philip Randolph.

Kennedy had sent a new civil rights bill to Congress because
of the pressure of the civil rights movement and felt that some
congressmen would get so angry with the marchers that they
would vote against the civil rights bill.

But none of the black leaders would agree. They believed that
the march would help ensure the passage of the civil rights bill.
In fact, they wanted one that was stronger than the one Kennedy had asked for.

Randolph told the president that blacks were already in the
streets, and they would not get out of the streets. He told
Kennedy that the leaders in the room wanted demonstrations to
be nonviolent. But he warned Kennedy that if they were not

listened to, if the government did not cooperate with them, then new leaders would arise who would be violent. And the president would have a lot more trouble dealing with such leaders. For already, some were saying that men like King and Randolph were too soft and that black people should arm themselves.

President Kennedy realized he had no choice but to agree. On August 28, 1963, the capital of the United States saw the largest demonstration in its history. Almost a quarter of a million people, black and white, people from all walks of life, but among them union workers, packed together at the steps of the Lincoln Memorial. Among those union members, of course, were Randolph's beloved Brotherhood of Sleeping Car Porters.

The first man to rise and speak to the crowd was tall and thin, a man who had been through more than 50 years of freedom struggles. He was, of course, A. Philip Randolph.

In his deep, strong voice Randolph told the huge crowd:

> Let the nation and the world know the meaning of our numbers.... We are the advance guard of a massive [great] moral revolution for jobs and freedom.... This civil rights revolution is not confined to the Negro, nor is it confined to civil rights, for our white allies know that they cannot be free while we are not, and we know we have no future in a society in which six million black and white people are unemployed and millions live in poverty....

Later on, it was A. Philip Randolph who introduced Dr. Martin Luther King, Jr., and then Dr. King began his famous speech which has gone down in history as "I Have a Dream."

It was the "most beautiful and glorious" day of Randolph's life. As the crowds slowly moved off at the end of the day, Bayard Rustin saw a lone figure still standing by the statue of Lincoln. He went toward the figure and saw it was Randolph. Tears were streaming down Randolph's cheeks. It was the first time that Rustin had seen him unable to control his feelings.

17 FATHER OF THE CIVIL RIGHTS MOVEMENT

" *I'll die with a hammer in my hand.* "

"John Henry,"
African-American folk song

Three months after the March on Washington, the news flashed to an unbelieving world that President John F. Kennedy had been shot to death! The country was in mourning. African Americans felt a special loss. They had come to see in Kennedy a friend, someone who had put the government firmly behind the freedom movement.

Lyndon Baines Johnson, the new president, and a southerner, promised to carry on the work of John Kennedy. Indeed, he did keep his promise. The Civil Rights Act became law on July 2, 1964. Now black people could not be kept out of schools, hotels, restaurants, or any other public places. Jim Crow laws and practices were now illegal. Another part of the law said that businesses could not discriminate against black people. On paper, Jim Crow was dead. But it would take years of struggle to enforce the new law.

Lyndon Johnson also saw a need to continue fighting a war in Vietnam. More and more money was pumped into the effort to win that war. More and more young American men were sent to fight it. More and more body bags were coming back.

Dr. King spoke out against the war in Vietnam, and so did A. Philip Randolph. People tried to persuade them not to do so. They were told it would hurt the cause of civil rights. They said it would look like black people didn't care about their country. But King and Randolph would not give in.

Randolph was now in his late 70s. He thought back on his life. He knew his struggles had left a mark on American history. But he was not satisfied. He wanted to leave something else behind, as well. He wanted to set up something that would keep going after he himself had passed away. And so, in 1964, he, the AFL-CIO, and a number of friends set up the A. Philip Randolph Institute. Bayard Rustin was named director.

The purpose of the institute was to be a center of ideas and action for helping to continue the work that Randolph had been engaged in all his life. The institute, for example, would be used to help take advantage of the new civil rights laws, to help train blacks in various job skills.

An important part of the early work of the institute was drawing up what was called Randolph's Freedom Budget for All Americans. This was a 10-year plan, drawn up by a team of both black and white economists and influential thinkers. The plan showed how the government in Washington could spend money for public programs to make sure that everybody got his or her fair share. But the government was not interested.

The institute now has 150 local chapters. Its members are from various black trade unions. Another of the institute's purposes is to serve as a bridge between the black community and the labor movement. Its goals are in keeping with Randolph's belief that black workers can exert political power.

*Protestors against the Vietnam War. A. Philip Randolph
spoke out against the war.*

Many honors were heaped upon A. Philip Randolph in his
closing years. Universities awarded him honorary degrees.
Streets were named after him. As early as 1942, the NAACP
awarded him its prestigious Spingarn Medal. In September
1964, President Johnson called Randolph to the White House.
This time it was not to argue with Randolph but to present him
with the highest honor this nation can bestow upon a civilian.
He was awarded the country's Medal of Freedom.

One would think it was time for Randolph to retire and take a much earned rest. But Randolph had not finished fighting yet. He felt the government should do something about making sure blacks could vote everywhere in the country. There were many places in the South where a black person would be taking his life in his hands if he dared to show up to vote.

In 1964, Randolph flew South to Selma, Alabama, to participate in the dangerous march to Montgomery alongside Dr. Martin Luther King, Jr. They were marching for the right to vote. The governor had vowed to stop that march. Many people expected bloodshed. Randolph was not strong, but he walked with his head held high. He was all right along the way, but on his way back to New York he fainted.

The march was a success. A watching Congress then went on to pass the Voting Rights Act in August 1965. This act pledged to use the U.S. Department of Justice to enforce the voting rights of black people. Federal examiners were to be sent to the South to register any black person who wanted to vote.

At about the same time, in the mid-1960s, racial riots broke out in the Watts section of Los Angeles, in Harlem, and later in Chicago, Detroit, and other cities. New black leaders, different from Randolph, emerged. They stressed exclusively black nationalism and black consciousness. And they did not rule out violence to accomplish their aims.

Randolph believed in nonviolence and in working together with whites for social justice. He criticized the rioters, the violent methods, and the ideas of exclusively black power and black business. Because of this, he earned the contempt of some of the new black leaders. They felt that the times had begun to pass him by, that he was out of step.

Randolph had lived through so many lynchings, so many assassinations, so much violence. But he was not prepared for the news in April 1968 of the assassination of the man he regarded as the towering giant of the civil rights movement, Dr. Martin Luther King, Jr. Dr. King had been gunned down in Memphis, Tennessee, while supporting a strike of black sanitation workers. It wasn't too long after that that John Kennedy's brother Robert, who was now running for president of the United States, was gunned down, too. Those were sorely trying times for Randolph, as they were for the whole country.

In September 1968, Randolph said good-bye to the Brotherhood of Sleeping Car Porters at their convention in New Orleans. Now 79 years old, he was no longer able to carry out the heavy duties expected of the president of the union, and so he resigned. As he was speaking to the convention, the Pullman Company was going out of business. It was the age of air travel, and the jobs of sleeping-car porters were fast disappearing.

One month after his 80th birthday, a party was held at the Waldorf-Astoria Hotel in New York City to honor the lifetime of work of A. Philip Randolph. Speaking in Randolph's honor were the great musician Eubie Blake, Mayor of New York John Lindsay, New York Governor Nelson Rockefeller, Roy Wilkins, head of the NAACP, and Mrs. Coretta Scott King, widow of Dr. Martin Luther King, Jr. Even George Meany had come to salute the man he had had so many arguments with in the past. Governor Rockefeller declared April 15, Randolph's birthday, as A. Philip Randolph Day in the state of New York.

On May 16, 1979, at the age of 90, A. Philip Randolph closed his eyes for the last time. In the casket, his face wore an expression of great sadness. Was it for his wife, Lucille, who had devoted her whole life to him and to his cause? Was it for the Kennedy brothers, John and Robert? Was it for Dr. King? Or had he been thinking of the tasks still undone?

As you walk west on 135th Street in Harlem, New York, you come to Morningside Park. Then, as you start climbing scores of steps that wind up a steep hill through the park, you will come across a building with high spires that dominate the surrounding area. That building, the A. Philip Randolph High School, is situated on the campus of the College of the City of New York where, seeking answers to all of life's great questions, A. Philip Randolph began his manhood journey.

Timetable of Events in the Life of
A. Philip Randolph

April 15, 1889	Born in Crescent City, Florida
1907	Graduates from the Cookman Institute in East Jacksonville, Florida
1914	Marries Lucille Campbell Green
1917	Begins publishing The *Messenger*
1925	Organizes Brotherhood of Sleeping Car Porters and becomes president
1936	Becomes president of National Negro Congress (NNC) Achieves acceptance of Brotherhood as full international member of AFL
1941	Organizes march on Washington, D.C., to protest discrimination in government jobs
1942	Holds massive rally at New York's Madison Square Garden
1946	Awarded Spingarn Medal by National Association for the Advancement of Colored People (NAACP)
1957	Elected vice president of AFL–CIO
1960	Elected president of Negro American Labor Council
1963	Directs massive march on Washington, D.C.
1964	Awarded the Medal of Freedom Founds the A. Philip Randolph Institute
1969	Honored with A. Philip Randolph Day in New York State
May 16, 1979	Dies in New York City

SUGGESTED READING

Anderson, Jarvis B. *A. Philip Randolph: A Biographical Portrait*. New York: Harcourt Brace Jovanovich, 1972.

*Bennett, Lerone, Jr. *Wade in the Water: Great Moments in Black History*. Chicago: Johnson Publishing, 1979.

Branch, Taylor. *Parting the Waters: America in the King Years 1954–63*. New York: Simon and Schuster, 1988.

Du Bois, W. E. B. *The Souls of Black Folk: Essays and Sketches*. New York: Fawcett, 1961.

Foner, Philip S. *Organized Labor and the Black Worker 1619–1981*. New York: International Publishers, 1982

*Greenleaf, Barbara Kaye. *Forward March to Freedom: The Story of A. Philip Randolph*. New York: Grossett & Dunlap, 1971.

*Hanley, Sally. *A. Philip Randolph, Labor Leader*. New York: Chelsea House, 1988.

Haywood, Harry. *Black Bolshevik: Autobiography of an Afro-American Communist*. Chicago: Liberator Press, 1978.

Morris, Aldon. *The Origins of the Civil Rights Movement*. New York: The Free Press, 1984.

Williams, Juan. *Eyes on the Prize: America's Civil Rights Years 1954–1965*. New York: Viking, 1987.

---

*Readers of *A. Philip Randolph: Integration in the Workplace* will find these books particularly readable.

SOURCES

BOOKS

Anderson, Jervis B. *A. Philip Randolph: A Biographical Portrait*. New York: Harcourt Brace Jovanovich, 1972.

Bennett, Lerone, Jr. *Wade in the Water: Great Moments in Black History*. Chicago: Johnson Publishing, 1979.

Davis, Daniel S. *Mr. Black Labor, Father of the Civil Rights Movement*. New York: Dutton, 1972.

Du Bois, W. E. B. *The Souls of Black Folk: Essays and Sketches*. New York: Fawcett, 1961.

Embree, Edwin R. *Against the Odds*. New York: Viking, 1944.

Foner, Philip S. *Organized Labor and the Black Worker 1619–1981*. New York: International Publishers, 1982.

Franklin, John Hope. *From Slavery to Freedom: A History of Negro Americans*. New York: Knopf, 1969.

Greenleaf, Barbara Kaye. *Forward March to Freedom: The Story of A. Philip Randolph*. New York: Grosset & Dunlap, 1971.

Hamilton, Virginia. *W. E. B. Du Bois: A Biography*. New York: Crowell, 1972.

Hanley, Sally. *A. Philip Randolph, Labor Leader*. New York: Chelsea House, 1988.

Haywood, Harry. *Black Bolshevik: Autobiography of an Afro-American Communist*. Chicago: Liberator Press, 1978.

Kempton, Murray. *Part of Our Time: Some Ruins and Monuments of the Thirties*. New York: Simon and Schuster, 1955

Miller, Spencer, Jr. *American Labor and the Nation*. Chicago: The University of Chicago Press, 1933.

Milton, Bruce, and John Stuart. *Men Who Lead Labor*. New York: Modern Age Books, 1937.

Osofsky, Gilbert. *The Burden of Race*. New York: Harper & Row, 1967.

Wilkins, Roy. *Standing Fast: The Autobiography of Roy Wilkins*. New York: Viking, 1984.

Williams, Juan. *Eyes on the Prize: American's Civil Rights Years 1954–1965*. New York: Viking, 1987.

MAGAZINE ARTICLES

The Messenger: World's Greatest Negro Monthly. Vols. 1–7 and 8–10, 1917–1928. New York: Messenger Publishing, 1917–1928.

RECORDINGS

"Great March on Washington" speech by A. Philip Randolph, 18/28-63. Motown Records, #H1261.

OTHER

March on Washington Movement—Proceedings of Conference Held in Detroit, September 26–27, 1942. The New York Public Library, New York.

"March on Washington Movement Presents a Program for the Negro: A. Philip Randolph." The Schomburg Center for Research in Black Culture, The New York Public Library, Newark. Microfiche 966.

INDEX

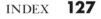

About the Author

Sarah E. Wright's first novel, *This Child's Gonna Live*, an African-American epic, was touted as "a small masterpiece" by the *New York Times Book Review*. She co-authored, with Lucy Smith, an illustrated book of poems called *Give Me a Child*. In addition, she has published a number of poems, book reviews, and articles in various journals. She is also a certified poetry therapist.

Born in Wetipquin, Maryland, Ms. Wright attended Howard University, Cheyney State Teachers College, the University of Pennsylvania, the New School for Social Research, Long Island University, and the University of the State of New York. She belongs to PEN, the Authors Guild, the International Women's Writing Guild, and other professional organizations.

Ms. Wright has received many awards for excellence in writing, including two MacDowell Colony fellowships for creative writing; the 1975 CAPS Award for Fiction from the New York State Council on the Arts; the 1976 Novelist-Poet Award, from the Institute for the Arts and Humanities at Howard University; the 1988 Middle-Atlantic Writers Association's Distinguished Writer Award; and the 1989 Zora Neale Hurston Award for Literary Excellence.

She is the mother of two grown children and lives in New York with her husband.

Excerpts from *A. Philip Randolph: A Biographical Portrait*, copyright © 1973, 1972 by Jervis B. Anderson, reprinted by permission of Harcourt Brace Jovanovich, Inc.

Picture Credits: A. Philip Randolph Institute: cover portrait, 20, 33, 41, 50, 63, 65, 69, 72, 94, 111, 115; AP/Wide World Photos: cover background, 115 (top); Culver: 79; Bert Miles 115 (bottom); Moorland-Spingarn Research Center; 47; Schomburg Center for Research in Black Culture, N.Y. Public Library, Astor, Lenox and Tilden Foundations: 9, 28, 60, 88, 104, 114, 117 (Laurance Henry Collection), 120.